Advance Praise for *Living Reading*

"This fascinating exploration of the lived experience of teachers provides important insights for teacher educators, administrators, researchers, and anyone involved in professional organizations. It reveals aspects of learning within organizations and of organizational learning itself that are crucial to understanding educational practice, but have rarely been studied systematically before.

In the book, Judith Davidson shares her sensitive and critical examination of the social practices of teachers as they participate within a professional organization and how those practices relate to their conceptions of literacy education. The writing reveals her deep understanding of issues in literacy research and pedagogy, but also of organizational practices and institutional change. Moreover, because her work depends upon careful discourse analysis, it requires a sophisticated conceptualization of discourse communities and intertextuality.

Many researchers have investigated teachers and their process of development, but few have looked deeply into the organizations beyond the school that provide the intellectual and social grounding for their work. The stories presented here will become a touchstone for future studies of teaching and teacher development."

Bertram C. Bruce, Graduate School of Library and Information Science,
University of Illinois at Urbana-Champaign

"Not every researcher has the gift of conducting a study of a particular instance or case and successfully transcending the particular to arrive at wise, broad understandings and insights. Judith Davidson has that gift. She conducted skillful and extensive fieldwork of reading councils, voluntary professional organizations. The result is an impressive, sophisticated, and nuanced book that draws upon the notion of communities of practice to reveal just how reading and the reading councils figure in the lives of the participating teachers. She arrives at the surprising conjunction of reading and spirituality and the generative conclusion of what it means 'to live reading.' In addition, the book is a good read."

Alan Peshkin, Stanford University

LIVING READING

STUDIES IN THE
POSTMODERN THEORY OF EDUCATION

Joe L. Kincheloe and Shirley R. Steinberg
General Editors

Vol. 124

PETER LANG
New York • Washington, D.C./Baltimore • Boston • Bern
Frankfurt am Main • Berlin • Brussels • Vienna • Oxford

Judith Davidson

LIVING READING

Exploring the Lives
of Reading Teachers

PETER LANG
New York • Washington, D.C./Baltimore • Boston • Bern
Frankfurt am Main • Berlin • Brussels • Vienna • Oxford

LIBRARY OF CONGRESS CATALOGING-IN-PUBLICATION DATA

Davidson, Judith.
Living reading: exploring the lives of reading teachers / Judith Davidson.
p. cm. — (Counterpoints; vol. 124)
Includes bibliographical references.
1. Reading teachers—Professional relationships—Illinois—Case
studies. 2. Reading—Illinois—Societies, etc.—Case studies.
I. Title. II. Counterpoints (New York, N.Y.); vol. 124.
LB2844.1.R4 D28   428.4'07—dc21   00-025187
ISBN 0-8204-4560-6
ISSN 1058-1634

DIE DEUTSCHE BIBLIOTHEK-CIP-EINHEITSAUFNAHME

Davidson, Judith:
Living reading: exploring the lives of reading teachers / Judith Davidson.
–New York; Washington, D.C./Baltimore; Boston; Bern;
Frankfurt am Main; Berlin; Brussels; Vienna; Oxford: Lang.
(Counterpoints; Vol. 124)
ISBN 0-8204-4560-6

Cover design by Mark Wickersham

The paper in this book meets the guidelines for permanence and durability
of the Committee on Production Guidelines for Book Longevity
of the Council of Library Resources.

© 2000 Peter Lang Publishing, Inc., New York

Printed in the United States of America

Contents

Acknowledgments

The first round of applause must go to the members of the local reading councils themselves. Without their help and assistance none of this would have been possible. My special thanks to Alan Farstrup, director of the International Reading Association; Susan Hanks, 1994-95 president of the Illinois Reading Association; John Logan and Paula Schoenfelder, IRC past presidents; Arlene Pennie, executive secretary of the Illinois Reading Council; and the many other unnamed but very present members of the association who were so generous with their time and thoughts.

Throughout the research effort, my dissertation advisor, Bertram Bruce, has been a critical force in shaping my understanding of these issues and inviting me to explore new avenues of thought. Each of my committee members—Liora Bresler, Alan Peshkin, and Daniel Walsh—has also made different and important contributions to the execution of this work. The willingness of "the dream team" to read, critique, discuss, and suggest has been greatly appreciated.

My thanks also to that special community of reading advocates in Indiana who have provided me with special insights on the work of local reading councils and, in particular, to Jack Humphrey, Linda Cornwell, Joan Lipsitz, and Jack McGovern.

From the inception of this work to its finish there have been many circles of professional friends who have provided special support, from my graduate school chums (Ann Larson, Lillie Albert, Jeanne Connell, Paula Shoppe, Anya Enos, Karen Smith, and Darias Kothawalla, among others) and my colleagues with the Hanau Model School Partnership (Elizabeth McNamara, Cathy Miles Grant, and Kevin McGillivray) to my colleagues and students at Boston College and the University of Massachusetts at Lowell.

My own family, while geographically distant, have been most encouraging, as have my extended family networks of Hasteds, Marleys, Hellers, and Jevickis.

Part I

INTRODUCTION, BACKGROUND, AND CONTEXT

Chapter 1

The Paradox of Reading

Amelia Bedelia is preparing to read. The woman playing the storybook character is dressed up in a maid's black dress and a crazy black hat with yellow flowers, like the character wears in the picture books. An older woman with thickly curled white hair announces the reader.

"Hello!" says Amelia Bedelia, stepping forward to the microphone. "How could you tell I was Amelia Bedelia?" she asks the children sitting in a circle around her, and then she begins talking about her hat. The microphone squeaks and squawks, making terrible sounds as she talks, but the children sitting near her seem to be able to hear.

A little boy raises his hand "I wanna win a book," he tells her.

She asks the children to name the Amelia Bedelia books they know and then says, "*Teach Us Amelia* is the one I'm going to read today. I'm so glad you're familiar with the stories by Peggy Parrish with me, Amelia Bedelia, as the main character."

The event described here is drawn from an observation at a mall of a "Read-In" sponsored by a local reading council, which I will call the Boxwood Council, an affiliate of the Illinois Reading Council (IRC), a group dedicated to promoting reading within its community. Amelia Bedelia's performance took place on a snowy Sunday afternoon in a Midwestern shopping mall. The stage is a carpeted pit surrounded by wooden benches in the center of the two-story mall. Children sit on the floor around Amelia Bedelia. Parents and other mall goers sit on the benches, stand around the edges, or peer over from the second-floor balcony. Many shoppers pass by without a second glance at Amelia Bedelia or the many tables of reading displays, but many others stop to look and chat with the teachers and volunteers, admiring children's artwork and flipping through the "shape" and "theme" books that children created in response to literature, social studies projects, or science inquiry. Supporters of local adult literacy projects pass out peppermint candies attached to flyers with program messages. Outside the mall entrance, mall goers may visit the bookmobile from the local library.

The Boxwood Council is one of twenty-seven local councils and seven statewide special interest councils that make up the Illinois Reading Council, an organization of some seven thousand members. IRC is itself a member of the larger International Reading Association (IRA), a group of some ninety-five thousand members, who live primarily in the United States.

Across our society there is a prevalent belief that learning to read is at the heart of all educational achievement. As a consequence, schools, researchers, policy makers, and community members place high value on the teaching and study of reading. Discussions of reading are often, then, discussions of education itself—its aims and its relationship to civic and economic life.

IRA is a voluntary professional organization representing those teachers with strong concerns about the teaching of reading. Many of their members are senior teachers, key players in the operation of their schools and central to many important facets of school decision-making and school culture. Through the course of this work, I was surprised to learn that researchers, despite their numerous and diligent efforts to understand the nature of reading and to improve educational achievement, have virtually ignored such voluntary groups of educators. This is unfortunate, as the study of such groups can provide vital clues to understanding reading as well as other areas of educational practice.

I spent one and one-half years observing and participating in four local reading councils that I will call Raven River, Boxwood, Illinois Heights, and Prairie. The four are located in central Illinois, an area of small- and medium-sized towns surrounded by expanses of corn and soybean fields. Several universities and colleges serve this region. At any one time there are between six hundred and eight hundred members on the rolls of the four councils. The majority of these members are elementary teachers and most, but not all, are female. A deep-seated belief in the importance of literacy and reading unites them, and integral to that belief is the belief that reading is what education is all about.

Because of the number and nature of positions that the members of these four reading councils occupy, as an organized group, what they think about reading and how they implement those beliefs may significantly shape classroom practice and, thus, children's school learning experiences. Understanding the reading belief systems that undergird council practice offers the potential for seeing more deeply than we have before into the ways teachers form and enact knowledge and values. However, understanding these beliefs and their roots requires a grasp of the context in which these ideas are rooted and have unfolded.

Understanding the Context of the Reading Councils

"There is widespread agreement that we as a nation must respond to the literacy challenge, not only to preserve our economic vitality but also to ensure that every individual has a full range of opportunities for personal fulfillment and participation in society" (Kirsch et al. 1993, x). We hear such statements about literacy frequently on radio, TV, and in the press. The same authors quote a study prepared by the American Society for Training and Development, which claims that "changing economic, demographic, and labor-market forces" are "creating a human capital deficit that threatens U.S. competitiveness and acts as a barrier to individual opportunities for all Americans" (Kirsch et al. 1993, x).

Warning bells about the dangers of illiteracy have resounded for decades in our society. More recently, these cries of danger, merging with concerns about declining educational excellence and our blunted competitive edge, can be seen at work within issues of national language and educational policy (Ruth 1991). Undergirding these cries of danger lies a foundational belief: language and literacy are critical aspects of national well-being. No matter how the discussion about language and literacy is constructed, this belief remains steadfast. For historical reasons, much of this concern about literacy focuses on reading (Monaghan and Saul 1987).

Reading instruction is seen as central to teachers' work, particularly the work of teachers of young children. This means that issues and concerns about reading, from selection of materials, organization of the classroom, and pedagogical approaches to assessment, professional development, and school policy, go right to the very heart of a teacher's work life and its unique rhythms and patterns, opportunities and restrictions. Teachers' livelihoods, professional autonomy, and their identities are bound up in the ways we think, describe, and act upon our concerns about reading.

Throughout this century, the history of the teaching of reading is filled with examples of teachers voluntarily organizing to deepen their personal knowledge base of reading or instruction, to act upon overlooked educational needs, to strengthen their professional field, and, not least, to enjoy the company of other teachers with similar concerns. These voluntary professional efforts take many forms, from independent reading groups and college courses to national professional improvement projects (like the National Writing Project) and professional associations (Goodman

1992; Shannon 1989; Squire 1991). Through voluntary assemblies, teachers solidify their opinions, explore their options, and engage in the ongoing work of defining themselves as teachers of reading. Voluntary groups can be agents of conservation or instigators of change.

Voluntary professional organizations have long played an important role in the development of ideas about language and literacy among teachers and other educational professionals. National organizations include the National Council of Teachers of English, the Modern Language Association, the International Reading Association, the American Library Association, and the Orton Gillingham Society, to name just a few. Each one occupies a particular philosophical or ideological niche, appealing to its own segment of literacy concerns, as well as drawing in people from other groups with overlapping interests.

These organizations have diverse strands of influence. They may promote professional development and community awareness through the formation of local groups, disseminate new ideas through broad publication programs, or influence policy through members' lobbying efforts or the employment of professional lobbyists. The meetings and conferences sponsored by these organizations, whether local, regional, statewide, national, or international, offer opportunities for concerned members to join their personal meanings of these issues with the social meanings attributed to them by the group.

As an example of the circle of this influence, consider this: school libraries everywhere possess a poster extolling reading, usually the product of either the American Library Association, the International Reading Association, or the National Council of Teachers of English. Every university library serving a college of education will have journals and professional publications from one, if not all, of these organizations in its collection. As a teacher, even if one is not a member of the organization, its influence reaches into your life in many ways.

Yet we know relatively little about these organizations. In regard to the International Reading Association, while there is some historical data, short of a few isolated and as yet unpublished studies, there has been virtually no research conducted on its affairs and operation, outside of its own marketing research and historical descriptions (Jerrolds 1977). At the time this study was conducted there was no descriptive or interpretive research available on what it is to be a member of such a group and how such participation contributes to individual and professional knowledge in the field. This lack of information about the role that educators' voluntary professional activities play in their thinking about reading represents a black hole of knowledge within reading research. The study of educators' voluntary professional activities offers a unique, unexplored vantage point for considering the world of reading and education—that of the teachers' chosen worlds.

Teachers choose to belong to these organizations; they are not forced to join. They organize their activities to suit their personal notions of appropriate professional behavior. By rights, the work that goes on in these organizations—its form and content—should represent what teachers believe is beneficial to educational practice and to their functioning as professionals. Accordingly, the study of teachers' voluntary professional activities provides us with a lens for viewing what teachers value, as opposed to what others believe teachers should value. These values are manifest not only in the conversations and writings of members, but also in the patterning and structure of their practice. If not all teachers elect to belong to such organizations, many of the most active members of school staffs do. Why they do so and what they feel they gain through that participation are important considerations of this study.

The Paradox of Reading

The episode of Amelia Bedelia at the mall is one activity among the many that compose the totality of the work of reading council members. Participation in such activities promotes either reading or the work of reading instructors, and it links reading councils across the state of Illinois to the state and the national organization, as well as to the work of schools, politicians, publishers, and businesses. Through their participation in the organization, members develop and articulate their beliefs about reading. The organization connects them to intricate networks of practice that encompass many realms of culture and enterprise.

The episode of Amelia Bedelia at the mall raises important questions about the meaning of reading as it is constructed by member educators, the role of the group in creating and shaping these meanings, and the relationship of out-of-school professional activity to in-school activities. What does this incident say about what reading council members believe to be true about reading and reading teachers? To go one step further, how might the views and values enacted here at the mall also be enacted in school practice?

Originally, I planned to explore the ways that ideas about literacy were formed and enacted through the practice of local reading councils. My emphasis was on these grassroots links in the organizational chain. In the course of this study, through my attendance at events like the "Read-in" at the Mall, I became increasingly aware that my preconception of what was a literacy belief and how it is "found" in practice hindered my understanding. I also became aware that the forms of reading research with which I was familiar could offer me only limited assistance in answering my research question.

As I entered the world of council practice, I realized I was not studying the act of reading as defined by most reading research, that is, something that is done with and to text. Therefore, I would not be able to "find" reading beliefs in the manner that I had anticipated. For many, my concerns about what I was learning fit better under the title of "organizational practice" rather than "reading theory." The more I learned about my subject, however, the less comfortable I became with this view. Beliefs about reading, members' ways of being, organizational structure, and the diverse settings and artifacts that council life encompassed—all seemed to be closely intertwined. In such a world, reading is a way of life, a set of interrelated meanings about the world and social activity.

Eventually I became aware of a paradox, best summed up as the tension between these two statements that I became familiar with during my research with the councils:

1. Reading is the thing that ties it all together.
2. We don't actually talk much about reading.

In many ways, the first statement represents for me the ways council members name their world. They place reading as the center point for understanding their world. The "it" in this statement refers to the world that one swims within as a council member, including the structure of the councils, the calendar of activities, and the ways councils are located in relationship to schools, businesses, and communities. This vast network of people and things is connected through the multiple meanings with which members imbue the word "reading."

In contrast, the phrase "we don't actually talk much about reading" represents for me the force of ideas that implicitly guide and shape council practice and that members work around and through notions of reading. These ideas are drawn from many sources, linking council life to the greater society in which it is embedded. These ideas run the gamut from the simple and practical, such as what is a good member and how should groups be formed and conducted, to more abstract concerns, such as how does my work contribute to a larger vision of society and in what forms might I speak of my participation.

For me, the paradox arose in coming to understand how both statements could be true. I found a solution to this paradox in the notion of "living reading."

Critical to me for making sense of this problem has been the concept of "communities of practice" (Lave and Wenger 1991). The reading councils are communities of practice embedded within and linked to various other communities of practice across our society. By community of practice, I refer to this formal definition: "A community of practice is a set of relations among persons, activity, and world, over time and in relation with other tangential and overlapping communities of practice. A community of practice is an intrinsic condition for the existence of knowledge, not least because it provides an interpretive support necessary for making sense of its heritage. Thus, participation in the cultural practice in which any knowledge exists is an epistemological principle of learning" (Lave and Wenger 1991, 98).

Knowing as and what reading council members know is predicated on participation. One learns to think as council members think by doing what council members do. For this reason, understanding the cycle of participation by which one enters, participates, and eventually leaves the fold of council life is critical to making sense of what it is that members believe about reading. The activities of the councils are the lens through which members learn to interpret the world and to imbue it with the values that council members hold dear.

Much of this practice is submerged in the sense that Bourdieu describes as "doxic" (Bourdieu 1977, 169). Socially informed members constantly move through spaces inscribed with meanings that they can read through the "senses" they have acquired as members of this particular world.

Communities of practice mediate their activities through symbols and rituals (McLaren 1986; Turner 1985, 1986) and through genre (Bakhtin 1986; Fairclough 1992), linguistic forms that provide recognizable vessels for the conduct of practice. As Bakhtin said of genre: "We learn to cast our speech in generic forms and, when hearing other's speech, we guess its genre from the very first words; we predict a certain length . . . and a certain compositional structure; we foresee the end; that is, from the very beginning we have a sense of the speech whole, which is only later differentiated during the speech process. If speech genres did not exist and we had not mastered them, if we had to originate them during the speech process and construct each utterance at will for the first time, speech communication would be almost impossible" (1986, 79).

As communities of practice, council members employ specific genres to conduct their practice, from the format of business meetings and the design of conferences to the preferred manner for public presentations. These genres dictate in part the form of the activity, the tone, and the expectations of participants. The notion of genre is of particular importance to my book, and in a later chapter I describe at length the ways genre, in the form of the expert presentation, shapes council practice.

Communities of practice are also distinguished by their discourse, that is, the "socially accepted association among ways of using language, of thinking, and of acting that can be used to identify oneself as a member of a socially meaningful group or 'social network'" (Gee 1989, 18). Through discourse, communities of practice create objects of knowledge and beliefs about the relationships that exist between them and define subjective positions (Foucault 1972). Within the councils, the discourse of the spirituality of reading, described in chapter 8, is a powerful shaping force.

Communities of practice are not islands of cultural continuity. They are vitally linked, generally overlapping, and may be highly permeable at various points. Meanings emerge at their interfaces. These meanings are often highly reflexive, and the transaction that produces them works subtle, and not so subtle, changes in all parties involved. For instance, as I describe in later chapters, councils borrow many of the trappings of other civic organizations with which they are familiar. The institution of "honor council," which is now a staple of council structure, was adopted from Rotary Clubs.

For these reasons, particularly important to my study is a theoretical notion of the permeability of the boundaries of community.

> In using the term community, we do not imply some primordial culture-sharing entity. We assume that members have different interests, make diverse contributions to activity, and hold varied viewpoints. In our view, participation at multiple levels is entailed in membership in a *community of practice*. Nor does the term community imply necessarily co-presence, a well-defined, identifiable group, or socially visible boundaries. It does imply participation in an activity system about which participants share understandings concerning what they are doing and what that means in their lives and for their communities. (Lave and Wenger, 1991, 98)

This definition creates an opening for considering the broadly diffuse kinds of communities of practice that encompass a discipline of thought like reading, and the variety of different roles to which educators within this discipline subscribe. It also provides a means of considering the ways the multiple levels of a loosely connected organization like a reading council incorporates people from broad geographical areas.

Schools, Spirituality, and the Reading Councils

Through the exploration of the paradox of reading described earlier, I came to learn that it is linked to another pair of issues that are equally important to the story I tell here, and that is the issue of the tension that exists between schools' structural concerns and what I have come to refer to as teachers' spiritual needs. Schools exist to fulfill the critical social charge to educate young citizens in the values and skills they will need to participate as members of our democratic society. To meet this charge, schools have evolved in particular organizational directions that define roles, tasks, schedules, materials, architecture, and many other items within their sphere. For better or for worse, these forms and structures sharply define participants' possibilities and opportunities. As I learned through this study, schools' structural and administrative forms often leave little space for addressing teachers' broad and complex spiritual needs.

By spiritual I refer to the many subjective and communal needs that individuals have for understanding who they are in complex circumstances and for acknowledging, nourishing, celebrating, and renewing themselves and their choices with others. How we feel, what we believe, and why we believe or feel so are spiritual concerns that touch upon our emotional, moral, social, and political values and behaviors. In schools, the spiritual refers to what it means to be a teacher, the values one embodies in that role, and the difficult choices thrust upon one, day after day. Teachers feel deeply the need to belong to thoughtful communities that will support and encourage them in their work, helping to replenish the emotional reservoirs that are drained through the demands of that work.

For council members, most of whom are women, the reading councils are special forums for spiritual acknowledgment and exploration. Certainly council members attend meetings and conferences in search of new ideas about reading and teaching, but, as important, they also seek inspiration, rejuvenation, and solace, and, in other words, a venue for expressing and fulfilling their spiritual needs. These forms of expression are shaped by the gender realities of the institution of education, the profession of teaching, and the organization of the reading councils.

In our society, there are numerous institutionalized ways of speaking and practicing one's spirituality. The most obvious example is the organized practice of religion, but discourses of spirituality also abound in popular culture. In council practice, talk of reading intertwines with these multiple discourses of spirituality. In this way, spirituality shapes notions of reading, and, in the end, reading becomes a form of spirituality. In other words, spirituality and reading mutually constitute each other. They draw upon shared worlds of symbol, ritual, roles, texts, and genres. In particular, however, Protestant forms of imagery and forms of practice are central to this construction of the discourse of reading as spirituality.

Just as in many religions, in council practice, reading represents a kind of church in which people "do" their religion, rather than talk about it. Members "do religion" by attending, tithing, and participating in the activities of the group. Doing the religion of reading is a matter of performing the rituals of the group and employing the symbols of its practice. Doing makes reading self-evident, and members feel little urge to talk about the "why" of reading. Living reading, then, is an expression of this state of being and thus dissolves the paradox between the two seemingly contradictory statements that I heard members make: (a) Reading is the thing that ties it all together, and (b) We don't actually talk much about reading.

Organization of the Study

The purpose of this study is twofold. First, it is my aim to describe the practice of the reading councils from the perspective of local councils and their members and to place this practice within a historical and contemporary context. In so doing, I aim to explore how through this practice members "live reading" and provide a thoughtful interpretation of this notion as it relates to the larger arena of education and theories about educational organization.

The study is organized into three parts. In part 1, I introduce the work and present my methodological assumptions and process. Here I also introduce the reading councils, their structure and goals, and discuss how they came into being.

In part 2, I explore the actual practices of the reading councils with focus on the local members and local council. I begin with the planning of the council year and then shift to exploring the notion of the "reading sorority" and members' shared beliefs and concerns. In "The Expert Presentation" I examine the primary genre of council practice, considering the ways that form and content are intricately linked. Part 2 concludes with a description of the end of the ritual reading council year—the annual reading conference.

I turn from local practice back to the wider angle view of the multiple levels of council practice and their implications in part 3 with a chapter on the discourse of the spirituality of reading. This is a unifying discourse that works across all levels of practice. The book concludes with a look at the implications of these findings for education and educational research.

Conclusion

At the heart of this work is the notion of the reading councils as communities of practice. The task of this work is to describe the world of the reading councils and, in the process, come to a deeper understanding of practical and symbolic meanings of the notion of reading—an idea that has long encompassed much of our hopes and concerns about education and our beliefs about the ways education can solve what we feel is right or wrong about our world.

Chapter 2

Coming to Know
the Reading Councils

At the outset of this study, I sought access to one of the local councils by presenting myself and my plans to Sarah Smith, a local council president. We met for lunch at a restaurant, and over lunch I learned more about this remarkable woman. Sarah is a mother and grandmother with over twenty years' experience as a teacher. Although she lives and works in a small rural town, she is worldly, having lived in a number of other communities and traveled frequently to all parts of the globe. Being a former nun, service to others is a principle by which she lives, and the reading council is only one of many local and national groups in which she participates.

She was friendly, inquisitive, and seemed generally interested in my study. This pleased me greatly. As I described my aims, I mentioned that this would be an ethnographic study. Sarah looked up from her plate, a bit puzzled by the term.

"Just what do you mean by ethnographic?" she asked.

"Some people call this qualitative research," I explained. "What I want to do is learn how to see the world like a reading council member. I just want to be present at all the events that council members attend so that I can understand what the reading councils are from the perspective of a member."

"Oh," she said quickly, her face brightening with understanding. "You mean like Margaret Mead?"

"Yes, like Margaret Mead." I said, relieved that we had managed to find common ground so quickly.

"Well, in that case," Sarah said with a perfectly straight face, "I think you should know that I have sex twice a week, preferably with strangers."

I experienced a sudden and horrible sinking feeling in my stomach. What had happened to our common ground, I wondered with despair. Is this what most people think anthropology is—the study of human sexual behavior? What would happen to my study if council members thought I really wanted to talk about sex while appearing to be interested in talking about literacy? Even in my wildest dreams I couldn't imagine a reading council member mentioning the topic of sex so casually, and certainly not a former nun. It took me some seconds to realize that she had been joking.

"Yes, Samoa must have been very interesting," I answered when I'd caught my breath.

This story says much about me as an ethnographer and the utter egocentricism of which the novice researcher is capable. I had assumed that a group organized to promote reading would focus primarily on that topic and that other threads of thought would seldom intermingle with the conduct of business around that topic. In so assuming, I expected that my needs should be the group's needs. I now realize that I was imagining their reading beliefs as fixed items that could be "discovered," something like shells that one could pick up off the beach.

This story also says something about the expectations that I held about the group and its membership. From my previous and limited contact with the group, I had created a picture of the membership—who they were, how they dressed, and how they thought—that was already firmly in place and guiding my behavior toward them. In this rather conservative picture, it was not possible that reading council members would make a remark of this sort. My thanks to Sarah for giving me an important lesson in open-mindedness and humility early in my research process.

This story also speaks to the preconceptions that qualitative researchers face in the educational field. Although many of the people we meet while doing research will not have deep knowledge of our research methodology, they will not be ignorant of it. Their conceptions of research will be drawn from knowledge of research in general (predominantly quantitative), perceptions of university researchers (bothersome and generally ignorant of what it means to work in schools), or awareness of "something like anthropology" (fed by specials on National Public Television and exposure to the National Geographic). Numerous assumptions follow from these bits and pieces of knowledge, all of which I met in one form or another. Probably most important for council members was the question, Is this kind of research valid? What will someone be able to say about who we are and what our practice means from this kind of research process? How will others judge it? How will we judge it? Validity and research methodology may be as important to the researchee as they are to the researcher and the research community.

Positioning Myself

Diversity reigns in the reading world. Its participants disagree about the best way to approach reading instruction, including the role of the teacher, the organization of instruction, the instructional materials, and the ways progress should be evaluated. There are those who see reading as a technical skill to be acquired by direct instruction of the different components of reading. Others take a more holistic or constructivist view, arguing for the diverse functions that reading can serve. These positions are both pedagogical and political; they are often simplified in a stereotypical manner.

I threw my support to the more holistic or constructivist positions when I was in the first grade, and I have wavered very little since then. My first-grade teacher, like most of her colleagues, assigned copious amounts of purple mimeographed reading work sheets, textbook publishers' products, designed to help us develop the skills we needed to master print. Even now in my mind's eye, I envision one of those purple-print pages before me: there is an m in the middle of the page, and my job is to draw a line from the m to everything else in the picture that starts with the same sound. I am drawing a line to "man," a picture of a white man in a suit, wearing a hat. He looks like the father in the "Dick and Jane" series. As soon as I completed one sheet, I had infinite more sets to do beyond that one. No matter how hard I worked I could never get beyond them.

As someone who enjoyed reading, I found the work sheets and the accompanying round-robin reading groups to be an incredible waste of time. After all, if teachers wanted us to read, why didn't they give us books like those at the public library, which I visited every week with my mother and brother and sister, and simply give us time to read. In the Portland, Oregon public schools of my youth, budget cuts had forced school library closures, and it was not until I was nearing the end of my grade school career that I had access to a school library. The elementary classrooms I attended had no libraries, only textbook materials and dictionaries for reading materials.

I did not like the basal reading exercises, and I soon found a way out of the boredom of endless reading work sheets. There was an empty desk next to mine. One day, I simply balled up the work sheet I was supposed to be working on and hid it far back in the recesses of the empty desk. I waited. Nothing happened. I did it once more. Again, nothing happened. Soon I was stuffing every reading worksheet that came my way into that desk. The teacher never seemed to notice that I was no longer doing them.

Then, disaster struck. One day, the first-grade teacher announced something called a "desk check." New to school and its routines I didn't know what this meant, but as I watched her progress through the room, I quickly got the drift. I was horrified. Always an obedient child, it now struck me that I had committed an unpardonable sin. Desk by desk, the teacher came closer and closer to me and my cache of unfinished reading work sheets. No bell rang mercifully to rescue me; the inevitable occurred. She reached my desk and discovered my infraction. I was ordered to remove each sheet and flatten it out again. It was quite a pile when I was done. Then came my object lesson. She selected the ones she thought would be most important for me to complete and they became this six-year-old's weekend homework.

I remember the sinking feeling I had as I left school that day, my arms filled with old reading work sheets. I thought with sadness of all the work I would have to do, instead of enjoying my family's visit to my grandparents' farm that weekend, where there were chickens and cows and a big hay-filled barn in which to play. There would probably not even be time to read my new library books.

An avid reader, I have always believed that one learns to read by reading. To do so, one must have access to all manner of reading materials and experiences that make meaningful links between the world and text. My beliefs in reading have much in common with Dewey's notions of art as vital, grounded in ordinary experience, and infusing experience with symbolic meaning (Dewey 1934). I would distinguish my strong support for reading, however, from those who promote reading for reading's sake—the "joy of reading" club. As you can guess, I have always been innately sympathetic to critiques of basal textbooks and, in particular, reading work sheets.

Despite my unhappy early school reading experience, I continued to enjoy reading, developing a deep interest in language and literature, an interest that over time became transformed into an interest in literacy, the social contexts of learning, and the social construction of knowledge. As a consequence of these interests, as a young adult I lived in Japan, studying Japanese language and literature, pursued an interest in Japanese children's literature, and eventually entered a master's program in reading education at Bank Street College of Education in New York City. Central to the Bank Street approach was an emphasis on rich, meaningful curricula, an emphasis that remains an important part of my educational outlook. At Bank Street I began the more formal development of my ethnographic perspective, first with their principles of child development and observation and later with the discovery of the ethnography of education.

From Bank Street I went on to develop an adult literacy program at the New York Public Library. At that time, writing process approaches were coming to the fore in the literacy world. At my literacy program site, we developed an approach that combined Bank Street's ideas about curricula and observation with a program that taught adults to begin reading through writing. Serving on the library's policy committee to integrate adult literacy programming across the vast library system, I began to develop an interest in the issues facing complex organizations. Through my position, I had the opportunity to meet hundreds of people with different stories and beliefs about literacy—from the students who were eager to gain literacy skills that had eluded them, to the educated volunteers assisting them, to the staff in libraries across Manhattan and the community groups I sought to involve in the project. Everyone had stories to tell about literacy, what it meant to them, why it was important, and how it should be learned. I was beginning to perceive the patterns and the variety in the stories they told and to make sense of them in an analytical fashion.

In 1986, I took a position as director of the Project on Adolescent Literacy at the University of North Carolina's Center for Early Adolescence, working on a national study of successful compensatory literacy programs for young adolescents in schools and community organizations. This project allowed me to travel around the country making observations and conducting interviews with educators in schools and community agencies. Again, I listened to the stories people told about literacy— what they believed, what they wanted their students to believe, and how they tried to meet those goals—and I watched what went on in their programs (Davidson and Koppenhaver 1993). Through these experiences I came to understand how important people's beliefs about literacy are to understanding their practice. I also learned that beliefs are framed in multiple ways within practice and that people's beliefs about literacy and the ways in which they are framed are constitutive of who they are and how they define themselves to others.

My links to the reading councils began through my membership in the International Reading Association (IRA) itself rather than a local council. Like many within their ranks, I was a "paper member," participating vicariously in the organization through reading their newspaper, *Reading Today*. In developing our professional collection at the New York Public Library, we ordered heavily from IRA's publication list, and in that way I became familiar with their book offerings. At the time, I felt that their publication list and journals focused more on specific instructional techniques and less on the contexts of learning in which those techniques were embedded.

In 1987, I attended my first IRA conference in Anaheim, California, to make a presentation on the literacy project. I did not like Anaheim itself and, perhaps coincidentally, was disenchanted in many ways with the conference. I was shocked by the crass commercialism of the exhibit hall and the ways the exhibitors infantilized their audience. I hungered for conversations about research and found little. Our presentation was slotted for the last session on the last day and only six people attended. I had never "done" a national conference before, and I felt like I knew no one. I had no notion of the numerous parties or receptions I had missed. I left feeling that I had somehow missed the point, socially and intellectually, and wondering where the heart of IRA was really located.

My connections with IRA continued, however, and later in my work at the Center for Early Adolescence, I had occasion to call on Alan Farstrup, then research director and now IRA executive director, to discuss the center's adolescent literacy projects. Notice of our literacy publications appeared in various IRA publications. I also served on an ad hoc committee on middle-grades reading issues that met once at the national conference. An important part of my job at the center was scanning every journal available that addressed middle-grades reading issues, a task that included IRA publications.

In 1989, through the Center for Early Adolescence I began to work with Jack Humphrey, an Indiana educator involved in the Lilly Endowment's Middle Grades Reading Initiative. Humphrey, a long-time IRA member, was responsible for much of IRA's phenomenal growth during the early 1960s when he served as national membership chair. Through his acquaintance I came to know more about the state and local organizations and to learn about the ways that the "little guy" teachers in rural and suburban districts around the country drew upon the organization for support. Humphrey's impressive longitudinal perspective helped me to understand how many changes and improvements in reading education had been introduced and channeled to members through the reading councils. He introduced me to the "worker bees" of his state's reading leadership, people who had quietly and surely made remarkable changes in programs and instruction and had influenced innumerable teachers. These were highly responsible, usually self-effacing, but subtly humorous and deeply loyal people. This layer of reading council activity had not been visible to me before.

In sum, I had for many years pursued an on-again, off-again relationship with the organization. I had developed a picture of the organization
as fair, friendly, but conservative, with deeper roots in cognitive
psychology's contributions to reading theory than in constructivist notions. It seemed to be an organization of a few genial older white men
(most of them administrators or university professors), many of whom
held leadership positions within the organization, and many older white
women (most of them elementary or Chapter 1 teachers), who composed
the bulk of the rank and file. Viewed en masse, they did not seem as
activist as the members of the American Library Association, nor as theoretically sophisticated as members of the National Council of Teachers of
English.

Over the years, I had gleaned a sense of the shape of IRA's organizational structure and, through my experiences with different branches of
the organization, had created a mental montage of members' outlooks
along several dimensions. I was of two minds in regard to the organization. On the one hand, I enjoyed the people immensely as friends and
colleagues and appreciated what they did on day-to-day basis for young
people. I applauded the support and acknowledgment the organization
offered teachers who might otherwise be isolated and adrift and respected
the political weight a group of that size could leverage on literacy issues.
On the other hand, I was aware of what I believe to be significant differences separating me from them, in many of our philosophical and political beliefs about literacy

Why IRA?

The questions that drive this study are the questions that have been puz-
zling me for many years: How is it that people, in particular educators,
construct knowledge about literacy? What are the parameters of that knowledge? How are their notions of literacy linked to other cultural notions,
such as ideas about religion or patriotism? What are the consequences
implied in different stances to literacy? I sought a research site that would
provide me with food for thought about these issues.

I considered a number of possible alternatives as the site of the study,
including schools, non-school agencies, publishers, national literacy initiatives, and other literacy organizations. In the end, I selected a handful
of local reading councils of the Illinois Reading Council (IRC), an affiliate
of the International Reading Association (IRA), as the location of my study.

This site appealed to me for several reasons. First, most members
were teachers; this would give me a window on school life and the mean-

ings of literacy that circulate therein. However, the organization was not restricted to teachers. Rather, it straddled a number of institutional and organizational boundaries, serving as a route for channeling various interests concerned with reading needs. Second, it was a voluntary organization, which meant that those involved had elected to participate presumably because they agreed with the goals and mission of the organization. Thus, what I would see there should reflect teachers' beliefs not mandated by school districts. Voluntary professional organizations offered a means of observing teachers "at work" when they were not at work, and I thought that this would provide a unique lens on instructional issues that had not yet been applied to this or other educational issues. Third, the central purpose of the organization was the promotion of reading or literacy, and I assumed it would therefore be easy to access their ideas on this subject.

Of great importance to me, IRC members seemed to represent the grassroots, unacknowledged teachers who, unlike a Jaime Escalante or a Nancy Atwell, will never receive national acclaim. Yet, they are concerned and hard working, willing to put in extra time to make things better for young people. These are the people who work thirty years in one district, and they are the people who stay in education when the going gets rough. To me, they are the backbone of educational reform initiatives, the ones critical to reach if reform is to be successful. I felt that we knew little about the ways they generate their ideas about reading and that this would be a good means of getting at that issue.

IRC or IRA was also a site that, I believed, would offer a unique view of the controversial issues in reading education. The organization, founded in 1955, grew to prominence during the glory days of reading research and instructional programs in the 1960s and 1970s, when cognitive psychology and its emphasis on the scientific study of reading still dominated. Reading, then, was often depicted as a technology or tool to be mastered or employed, and instruction emphasized the breakdown of the skill components. This outlook found close allies among basal textbook publishers, and many of the leaders of IRA, such as William S. Gray, were also prominent authors of basal textbook series. It was this kind of instruction that I had encountered in my first-grade class in 1960.

Today, the community of reading educators is in great flux. Their very philosophical foundations are now under siege. Constructivist notions of reading and education challenge some of the most sacred tenets, such as "reading is the foundation of all learning." As assumptions about reading evolve, so too must assumptions about classrooms, materials, and those who teach reading. People long active in the organization say that it used to be so simple; that is, they knew what the organization was about, and what it was about was reading. Now unsure of the mission of the organization, they are unsure of what reading really is. They worry about the fragmentation of the field, but also about the many other educational issues, such as assessment, site-based management, and restructuring, which dominate discussions and draw the spotlight away from reading. Selfishly, I realized that their quandary represented an opportunity for me, as it might force important issues to the surface that would, under less stormy conditions, lie submerged.

Specific Methodological Issues

For educational ethnographers, the ethnography of schools represents the textual exemplar of our practice. The narrative form it takes is deeply ingrained in our consciousness, although we may not be aware of this until we confront it, as I did in this study. The "master narrative" presented in the school ethnography obtains much of its classic shape from the geographic, architectural, and temporal structure of schools as we know them. Schools occupy a defined physical location. The buildings in which they are housed are patterned in a limited number of ways. We can expect a playground, gym, office, classrooms, library, bathrooms, and halls. The school year unfolds in a ritualistic cycle, the rhythms of which often parallel the ethnographer's cycle within the school. The ethnographer's narrative of coming to know, learning and growing, and leaving the field are sung in the same key as the school calendar with the same harmonies.

In schools, labor and attendance are compulsory matters. Teachers are under contract. While many enjoy their work, they nonetheless are employees. Their participation in various parts of school life may not be voluntary or to their liking. Students are required to attend school. They have no choice in the matter. Thus, the communities that form within schools often coexist with contradictions.

Because we are so familiar with what can be expected from schools— how they will look, what positions staff will occupy, and how we will talk about them—it is not difficult to confer anonymity upon them. When we say "an elementary school," the reader or listener has an immediate picture. Although we know that schools vary greatly and that the purpose of a good ethnography is to bring forth the particular, the term "elementary school" still conjures up a picture believed to have intersubjective agreement.

The organization I studied offered many contrasts to the "master narrative" of educational ethnography as it is embodied in the school study. The organization does not exist in one identifiable place. It takes place in many geographical and architectural milieus, from hotels and restaurants to malls, homes, and schools. It occupies a temporal geography that surrounds and penetrates school life, but never encompasses it. Events occur after school, on weekends, or on special teacher leave days. The council calendar has an episodic flavor, as compared to the continuous and routine sense of time that schools exude. Members must find time around their job and home duties in which to conduct their organizational work. Because this is a volunteer group, people elect to join and leave at their own volition. They are not required by their position to be part of the group, and they cycle in and out in response to personal needs and attachments.

The seemingly deeper sense of recognition that we believe we possess of schools allows us to present them as anonymous structures, but I found that we lack commonly accepted terms and images by which to confer anonymity on an organization such as the one I studied. The terms "literacy organization" or "reading council" brought forth confusion when I tried to use them without further explanation. In addition, while there are numerous elementary schools across the nation, there is only one International Reading Association, and its unique perspective is critical to this story.

As a consequence of these differences, I had to take up a position of semi-anonymity in relationship to my topic. I do not hide the fact that it is the Illinois Reading Council (IRC) and the International Reading Association (IRA) that are the organizational framework within which my study rests. These entities are identified by name, but within them I extended anonymity to the local councils and their members with whom I have worked. In this way, I hope to be able to provide an accurate sense of the public context within which the local councils work, while respecting the privacy of individual members and local groups. For this reason, all references to the names, locations, and individuals working in local councils have been camouflaged. I have also changed the names of individuals working at the state level. In some cases, I refer simply to individuals by their position. The names of local speakers have also been changed in order to preserve the anonymity of the local group, but the names of authors and other public figures, where appropriate in the discussion of state- and national-level events, have been retained.

The dilemma I faced in deciding this issue raised many questions in my mind about the notion of anonymity and its depiction in the methodological literature. Ethnographers opt for anonymity so that in our magnanimity we can protect the innocent, but I wondered if there was also another side to that perspective. It seemed that anonymity also conferred absolute rights to the story on the researcher by refusing to name the researchees and to allow others the basis for rebuttal. Was anonymity a paternalistic, but nevertheless highly controlling manner of protecting the exclusive rights of the story for researchers?

This concern was raised in my mind by recent publicity about the changing norms of adoption and surrogate parenting. The classical approach to adoption has been to require absolute secrecy of the child's parentage, a position that has begun to change over the last few years as more adopted children demand the right to know who their birth parents are, and as more birth parents ask for information about the lives of the children they gave up for adoption. In many ways, the classical ethnographic position resembles that of the classical position on adoption. Social workers or courts, that is, experts, controlled the rights to the story and the voices of other significant parties were silent or only allowed restricted roles in the official record. Like social workers and courts, ethnographers have sought over the last few years to rectify their position. But what is interesting is that while ethnographers have attempted to diversify the voices they present in the story, making greater efforts to capture the complexity of the story, to the point of including the rebuttal and response of the other, they have not yet given full consideration to naming "the other."

In developing my semi-anonymous stance, I drew upon both ethnographic and journalistic standards about the line between private and public materials and the manner in which one represents others. I have not solved the problem I raised, and in many ways I've probably complicated matters. Partial naming may be no answer at all, but I am committed to continuing to explore the issue and its implications.

Before I approached the local and state IRC officials for permission to study their organization, I thought carefully about the way I would present myself and my project and the way I would tell my "cover story." I worried about my own semi-anonymous status with IRA. Although I was not acquainted with people in IRC, I had many contacts in other parts of the organization. The people whom I knew in different parts of the organization knew me, however, not as a graduate student researcher, but as a published author and advocate for adolescent literacy issues. I had no way of knowing what IRC members might learn about me if they spoke to people who were familiar with me, or how that information might color the future of my project. My stance, I determined, would be that of a graduate student, a novice to their organization, and someone desirous of learning from them. I would not be author, advocate, or evaluator. I would not hide my background from them, but I would avoid bringing it to their attention. If asked about my background, I would answer honestly, but briefly, seeking to return the discussion to their interests.

There were a number of issues regarding my stance as a researcher, and although I anticipated them at the outset, I did not have a realistic sense of their importance until I was involved in the project. For instance, there was the issue of the complicated relationship that educators possess toward research and researchers versus non-researchers and universities versus schools, particularly the relationship of Illinois reading educators to the University of Illinois. Reading council members hold the University of Illinois and its Center for the Study of Reading in the highest respect, particularly in regard to the names associated with the center's work, particularly those of P. David Pearson and Richard Anderson. I hadn't taken classes from either one of these professors; however, I was still, by virtue of my enrollment at the University of Illinois, circulating within their realm and for this reason considered very privileged: an honor I had to uphold.

Members' positions toward researchers and research are contradictory, composed of both respect and disdain. One distinguishing mark of council practice, members believe, is the importance they attribute to basing their practice on research. The councils, through the local presentations and the statewide conference, provide members with opportunities to learn about research. Frequently, presenters at council events refer to "the research," or claim that "research proves" something. Although their use of the term "research" and the rhetorical ways that they refer to research findings are structured in different ways than they would be by scholars, these references are a critical aspect of the validation of their practice.

Along with the current of respect, however, is an equally strong current of disregard for researchers whom they believe have no idea of what it is to work in a classroom under normal conditions, not to mention what they believe to be the increasingly difficult conditions of modern school life. "Have you ever taught?" I was asked with some sharpness by several members. Once, when I answered that I had taught second grade for one year, a woman told me, "That's a good thing, because a lot of those people at the university have no idea what it is like to be in the classroom." At a banquet, when I introduced myself to my tablemates and said, when asked, that I was not a teacher, one demanded of me, "If you're not a teacher, what are you doing here?"

Their concerns about researchers and research were not only about research in general, but also specifically about my research. They understood that experience critically shapes what one sees and learns in a situation. Clearly, they were concerned about the eyes with which I looked. Would I have the necessary skills to see and hear the realities of teachers, or would my researcher stance draw me too far away from their world for it to make sense?

I had to craft a position for myself, not only as a researcher, but also as a woman. Most of the organization's members are older, female, married, and parents. They juggle numerous family responsibilities in addition to their work and community service. During their meetings and in their casual conversation they make frequent reference to husbands, children, and parents (who may also need care). The few who are not married have their classrooms, which may fill a similar role in dealing with married colleagues. Not having a spouse or children (mine or a classroom of other people's children) could have made me suspect in their eyes as someone who would not have the proper experiences or responsibilities to be able to understand their world, and I had to search for ways to appear normal despite these "handicaps." In casual conversation I focused on our similar interests in weight, health, food, gardening, and children's books. Where males would talk of sports, I found that outside of walking and the occasional member who did aerobics there was little interest in talking of exercise or team sports. I learned quickly that speaking of my growing passion for ice dancing dampened rather than opened conversational opportunities.

It was not only council members who constructed me based upon their knowledge of my singleness and childlessness, I was surprised to learn the extent to which I constructed myself by these terms. A council member speaking to me of her older adolescent children and their familiarity with electronic equipment said to me, "That's how they grew up. It wasn't like that for us." I started, surprised that she had considered me part of her age cohort, because until that moment I hadn't considered her part of mine. And yet, I realized, we were exactly the same age. It was I who had constructed us as different, working under the assumption that I was somehow not as old as she because I didn't have grown children or own a home. It was not only that I had constructed her as a different age and generation, I had constructed her as a different kind of woman from myself because of these entailments, emphasizing the differences rather than the similarities between us. This incident made me aware of the dual nature of construction and the ways it might be at play in my discussions with council members.

Heading into my work, I gave careful consideration to the ways that I might reciprocate to members for their assistance and the ways my work might benefit their goals, not just mine. This has been a concern of mine throughout the project, and it is an area in which I have continually questioned myself. Unlike a school ethnography, where access is negotiated with the school's leader who obligates the staff to participate, I was seeking their indulgence and time not only after school, but also beyond what they had planned to give in service to their volunteer organization. I felt guilty asking them for this time, knowing in my heart of hearts that the powerful service ethic by which they lived would goad them to do it. I felt relieved, then, by the personal excitement my interviews generated among members. Several told me that they enjoyed the interview process, and one shared that it had helped her in formulating her plans for council activities. I also made gifts of food whenever possible, such as bringing a batch of brownies to a planning meeting. When members sought information on a topic, such as simple ways to bind books, I shared my resources, sending xeroxed articles that I thought would be helpful. Where appropriate, I helped with the physical arrangements for events, folding chairs and carting them to different locations, picking up and throwing away debris from refreshments.

The question of reciprocity raises the question of where and how one draws the line between researcher and researchee, and the relationship one assumes between participation and observation. As a participant, I was conscious only to perform the more menial tasks that any member could perform. I did not want to put myself in the expert position, using the specialized skills I had developed in my previous work. In so doing, I emphasized my observer role. As the study wound to an official close, however, I found myself erasing that line between participation and observation, crossing back and forth with greater ease. When I attended meetings, such as the statewide strategic planning meeting, I offered the group information about what I have learned from studying them, information that I thought would be helpful for them to consider in making their future plans. I willingly worked with small groups, talking as freely as a member would about the ideas under discussion, or writing out a position for the group. Ironically, I sense that my expertise or skills might have been suspect if I had simply entered the group as a participating member—they smacked too much of the world of non-schools, foundations, universities, and other entities. Having had more than a year to come to know me, however, they now accepted these skills and experiences with greater ease.

Council members at all levels consider their business to be public and believe themselves to be honest, straightforward people who speak their mind regardless of who is present. For these reasons, they welcomed me to observe their public meetings, as well as their more private planning meetings. "Everything we do is public," I heard frequently. In a legal sense, this is true, but in a more realistic sense there is much that occurs even in public meetings that they would consider private. I was always aware of the line that I walked between public and private and the rights and responsibilities I incurred through that knowledge.

Data Gathering and Analysis

I began the project with a pilot study, which I conducted during the spring of 1993. During that time I volunteered weekly doing clerical work at IRC headquarters in Bloomington, Illinois, and making observations of one local council's planning meetings and public events. I also attended the statewide reading conference that spring. I will be forever grateful to the generosity of IRC secretary Arlene Pennie, a cheerful and knowledgeable woman, and I looked forward with eagerness to my three hours with her at IRC headquarters every week.

In June 1993, I visited IRA headquarters in Newark, Delaware, for three days. There I toured the building, developing a picture of the physical plant, the divisions, and the people. I also spent time researching in the library and conducted interviews with the leaders of the organization. The staff were friendly and helpful, and I was grateful for their willingness to spend time talking with me despite their busy schedules. Indeed, IRA staff exhibit the same characteristics that members at all levels of the organization deem to be so important—friendliness, a strong belief in the work ethic, a positive attitude, and the faith in the importance of their mission.

It was through these experiences that I developed my data gathering and analysis plan in greater depth. For this study I have used a triadic data acquisition framework that includes interviews, observations, and textual/semiotic artifacts and their analysis. Interviews and observations provide traditional ethnographic materials, and, in fact, one could say that ethnographic accounts are dominated by their presence. When ethnographers gather textual and/or other semiotic artifacts, however, they most often use them as adjunct descriptive materials, subsidiary to the primary materials. In this work, I sought to give equal weight to all three types of data. This was particularly important since much of the organization exists, and is enacted, on this textual plane. Many members are, as I once was, "paper members," whose entire knowledge of the organization is based upon the materials that they receive from it in the mail.

Observations

The pilot work helped me to develop the parameters of the study. I decided that my focus would be the local councils. Two local councils would be my primary focus and two more local councils would receive more scattered attention from me. For the two main councils, I attended all planning meetings and all public events during the 1993–94 school year. For the peripheral councils, I attended a planning meeting and a public event. Of the two councils I picked for the closest attention, both drew most of their members from dispersed suburban and rural districts. One of the groups met monthly and sponsored five public events during the year. These events included afternoon presentations that would draw an audience of seventy teachers to a special half-day conference with hundreds of participants. Many of their efforts required coordination among many members, as well as support from local school districts and community groups. The other group sponsored three evening meetings during the year. This group met sporadically, and their affairs required far less long-range and comprehensive planning.

I also attended IRC Board of Directors monthly meetings; local council presidents, as board members, also attended these meetings. In addition, I also elected to attend IRC Executive Committee meetings to get a better sense of the connections between that group and the board of directors. Local members also link to IRC through the state conference, which I attended in 1993 and 1994. In addition, it was my luck that the Midwestern Regional IRA conference was sponsored by IRC in 1993 and held in Illinois, a once in a decade event that I also attended. In 1994, I attended the IRA conference in Toronto, Canada.

Where appropriate, I took copious notes of the events, as they progressed. I was fortunate in that taking notes at meetings could be a natural act for any member. I translated these scratch notes into field notes, as soon as possible after the actual event. They now compose a corpus of several notebooks of neatly typed pages.

As I mentioned earlier, reading council activities are episodic compared to the day-in, day-out nature of the school routine, and I often had to drive some distance to participate. (I've put thousands of miles on my car in pursuit of council activities). Although these activities are physically and temporally on the periphery of members' lives, it would be wrong to assume that the practices of the group are also peripheral or extraneous to their ideas about education in general and reading in particular. The very opposite is true, I believe.

Interviews

In addition to the observations I conducted, I interviewed a broad range of members. Because my focus was on the local council member, it was important to have strong representation from members who were currently active at that level. I sought out people at several stages of their volunteer career within the organization—those who had elected to stay on the sidelines, those entering greater leadership roles, and those who had cycled out of leadership roles. In order to gain greater knowledge of the local councils and their relationship to the state councils, I interviewed members who were now active at the state level, but at one time had been active local members. At IRA headquarters I interviewed the leaders of the organization, as well as a former IRA president and board member. I spoke with both women and men. I also sought out members who might give me different perspectives on controversial concerns within the organization. In total, I conducted thirty-nine formal interviews, twelve with men and twenty-seven with women. My sample included one African American member.

Time and geography presented complications for interviewing, as they did for conducting observations. I found that while some interviews could be scheduled in conjunction with council events, for many members, telephone interviews were a far better alternative. These formal interviews lasted for forty-five minutes to one hour and were loosely structured around the format of my written protocols. Through the interviews, I learned about members' history in the organization, the mode by which they came to participate, their beliefs about reading and the mission and purpose of this group, and their feelings about the membership and their role as a participant. I also questioned them about their work with IRC and IRA. Each interview was taped, including the telephone interviews, and transcribed; and transcribed copies were returned to the interviewees for their further comments.

I did not, officially at least, conduct multiple in-depth interviews with this group of participants. I thoughtfully considered this possibility when I began but found that unlike the school ethnography that I had worked on the year before, I did not have the deep organizational understanding that would allow me to sketch out this longer format before I started. Without some sense of foreknowledge about where I was going, I was hesitant to commit myself, or them, to multiple meetings, particularly in light of the time and geographical constraints we faced. It was only later in the process that I realized that I could have created a more open-ended and evolving discussion that would have served a similar goal for me. This did occur naturally for me in several cases, where people with whom I conducted a formal interview continued to come to me to discuss the issues raised in our interview as well as to discuss emerging issues in council life. This development helped to free me to see possibilities for the use of the multiple in-depth interview, possibilities I had not before seen.

Ethnographic Log

According to Sanjek, "Ethnographic validity may be assessed according to three canons: theoretical candor, the ethnographer's path, and fieldnote evidence" (1990, 395). My ethnographic log has been critical to me for charting my path as an ethnographer and linking theory with practice. I began the log during the pilot study, as part of a class assignment, and continued it throughout the next year. At the more intense parts of the process I wrote in it almost daily, keeping it open on my desk so that I could easily jot down a new idea or concern. In preparation for beginning the final stages of writing, I indexed the contents of the three and one-half volumes I now possess, separating issues into questions or observations about general theory, ethnography, and the councils. I was surprised by the number and depth of the issues that I had covered in these daily jottings. Just as scratch notes are the basis of fuller field notes, my ethnographic log became the basis of my later memos on various topics.

Textual/Semiotic Analysis

As mentioned before, much council participation occurs on "paper." Each local council with which I interacted produced its own newsletter. These are ephemeral documents, often a cross in format between a newsletter and flyers. Publication times are flexible, dependent upon publicity needs. Few groups publish more than four times a year. Each local council member also receives *The Communicator,* IRC's statewide newsletter distributed four to five times a year, and the *Illinois Reading Council Journal* (IRCJ), published four times a year. One of the most widely used documents produced at the state level is the annual conference program.

Basic membership to the IRA includes a copy of their substantial bimonthly newspaper, *Reading Today.* Members may also elect to receive *The Reading Teacher,* a journal for elementary teachers, *The Journal of Reading,* for teachers of students at higher levels, *Reading Research Quarterly,* or *Lectura y Vida* for Latin American members. IRA also

maintains a publications division that produces numerous books on topics of interest to reading educators.

For the purposes of this study, I collected the newsletters from all four
local groups that I had identified as my focus. In addition, I received all
issues of *The Communicator* published during that period, as well as
amassing a semi-complete collection of earlier copies going back to September 1981. I have copies of the 1993 and 1994 conference program.
I also received all copies of *IRCJ* published during this period. From IRA
I received *Reading Today,* and in order to have a contrasting perspective
on these documents I also subscribed to the National Council of Teachers
of English newspaper, *The Council Chronicle.*

In addition to these documents, through relationships with IRA or the
sale of membership lists, council members also receive many other kinds
of materials that I also added to my document files. These include calls for
credit cards, insurance, or special travel offers, among others. At conferences and other meetings, members also receive many "freebies," from
flyers, catalogs, and postcards to posters, T-shirts, and pens and pins. I
have collected many of these other artifacts as well. Finally, I have taken
many, many photographs of council events, particularly exhibits, in order
to document the numerous texts, symbols, and symbolic arrangements
that convey ideas about literacy to members.

Analysis

Analysis, which sadly was conducted in the old cut-and-paste method,
prior to the advent of software packages for data analysis, has been ongoing throughout the study. I read and analyzed field notes early on, developing emergent category codes as I proceeded. For my purposes, I found
it more helpful to create an analysis memo for each set of field notes
related to one event, rather than one large, coded document. In these
individual memos, I would categorize and index all the items under the
category codes and develop emerging themes in a following section. I
found that indexing my notes this way helped me to get to a finer-grained,
more thoughtful level of analysis than I might have by other means.

Using my analysis memos and notes from my ethnographic journal as
a basis, I wrote numerous memos about issues that were emerging as
important concepts in the study, issues which eventually formed the basis
of the dissertation and its organizational themes.

In undertaking discourse and/or semiotic analysis, the works of
Buckingham (1993), Lutz and Collins (1993), Radway (1984), and van
Dijk (1993) have been of particular importance to me. In addition, I was

extremely lucky to be able to attend the Sociolinguistics 10 Symposium in Lancaster, England, in April 1994, where I saturated myself in notions about discourse and its analysis. This is where I encountered the work of Fairclough (1992) in critical discourse analysis and that of Kress (Hodge and Kress 1988) with his interest in discourse and semiotic analysis.

The discursive analysis I designed for this project borrows from many of these places. For each newsletter in my collection, at the local and state level, I conducted an overall analysis of content and specific features, an analysis which I then used as the basis for a consideration of content themes and features that thread throughout each level. For an analysis of *Reading World,* IRA's bimonthly newspaper, I selected two issues (February/March 1993 and August/September 1993) for close comparison. For each issue, I created a summary memo of topics and contents with notes on format; this memo was complemented by a subject index memo. From this base I made an overall analysis of topics, themes, and format issues for each issue and comparatively across both issues. In addition, I also conducted a comparison of front page articles, photos, and formats for the six issues of *Reading Today* and *The Council Chronicles* published in 1993.

My most comprehensive analysis evolved around the 1993 and 1994 state conference programs. I examined the contents of sessions presented, the relationship of highlighted to non-highlighted sessions, presenters' affiliations, rhetorical strategies used across the text, and the relationship of text to photos and graphics. I also compared differences between the 1993 and the 1994 conference as presented in the program. I did a rough analysis of the 1994 IRA program catalog to provide myself with another contrastive lens for viewing the state conference.

For the purposes of this study, I focused my attention on my analysis of the textual and semiotic materials. In another time and place, however, I think it would be useful to investigate more deeply how the audience of these messages receives them and what meanings they construct from them.

I completed the study in 1995 and the book in 1999. In the interim, I was engaged in another qualitative study, an investigation of full-school technology integration in a kindergarten through twelfth-grade cluster of four schools. As a consequence of that work, I had the opportunity to delve deeply into issues about the technology of schooling (of which literacy and texts are crucial elements) and concerns about educational reform and teacher professional development. This subsequent study contributed much to the development of this book and my evolving thinking about the methodological and substantive issues presented here (Wasser 1998; Wasser, McNamara, and Grant 1998).

Researching in the Feminist Genre
This is not a feminist study. It is, rather, a study researched in the feminist genre, a term I borrow from my graduate school colleague Theresa Vasconcelos. "In the feminist genre" is a comprehensive term, embracing subjects and topic of the study, the researcher, and the mode of conduct for the inquiry. By this I mean that the organization I am studying is primarily composed of women working in a profession in which women compose the majority. For these reasons alone, gender issues must be present and thoughtfully considered. In addition, I, the researcher, am female, and, as I have described earlier in this chapter, gender consider-ations were present as I negotiated my role in the organization. Concerns about who I am as a woman in this culture in relationship to other women figured importantly in my reflections about my subjectivity.

Finally, researching in the feminist genre also implies special concerns related to the conduct of research (Weedon 1987).

Conclusions

Throughout the course of this work, I have found myself fascinated by the ways that talking, seeing, and reading are transformed through brain and pen. The process raises more questions perhaps than it answers, such as the "master narrative" of the school ethnography, the patriarchal inter-pretation of the concept of anonymity, or the importance of texts to ethnography, particularly in a literate society.

This process of interpretation is an intensely personal one. I am often conflicted about my constructions of the group and my loyalties to it. At the same time that I have felt great friendship, interest, and sympathy with council goals and outlooks, there have also been times when I was inordinately bored with proceedings, dismissive of outcomes, and critical of intentions. Regardless of the passion of the moment, I have sought at all times to maintain a commitment to respect.

Chapter 3

What Is a Reading Council? Why Reading?

When I began this study and was queried about it, I would explain, "It's about the reading councils." Invariably, the next question would be, "What's a reading council?" As I delved more deeply into organizational history, I, too, had my own reoccurring question—why reading? The first question refers to the contemporary structure of the organization, its activities, and aims. The second question refers to the historical context of its development and the implications of that development. In this chapter, I attempt to answer these two very basic questions.

What Is a Reading Council?

The reading councils are a conglomorate of legally chartered organizational nonprofit entities, encompassing local groups, state organizations, and the national umbrella organization—the International Reading Association (IRA).[1] Members are fond of describing the organization as a pyramid, with IRA at the pinnacle, the state organizations just below them, and the local organizations representing the broad, unshakable foundation.

Purpose and Goals
Just as the organizational structures at the state and national levels mirror each other, so, too, do the purpose and goals. At the IRA level, the goals are stated in this manner:

Nature:
The International Reading Association shall be a professional organization of individual and institutional members who are concerned with the improvement of reading and the development of literacy.

Purpose:
1. To improve the quality of reading instruction at all levels
2. To develop an awareness of the impact of reading among all peoples
3. To promote the development among all peoples of a level of reading proficiency that is commensurate with each individual's unique
   capacity. (International Reading Association 1992)

The essence of the goals for the Illinois Reading Council (IRC) is well
captured in the mission statement that appeared in the 1993 IRC annual
conference program: "The mission of the Illinois Reading Council is to
strengthen the quality of reading and related literacy instruction. The ultimate goal of the Illinois Reading Council is empowering individuals and
adding pleasure to their lives through reading" (1993a).

This mission statement is elaborated upon in the organization's bylaws
under the section headed "purposes."

A.   To improve the quality of reading instruction at all levels.
B.   To sponsor conferences and meetings planned to implement the
     purposes of the council.
C.   To act as a coordinating agency for all councils and to encourage
     the formation of new councils.
D.   To act as an intermediate clearing house for information related
     to reading.
E.   To cooperate with the Illinois State Board of Education in im-
     proving standards.
F.   To stimulate and promote research in the field of reading.
G.   To serve as a liaison agency between the IRA and all councils
     within the State.
H.   To further all purposes of the IRA.
I.   To disseminate knowledge helpful in the solution of problems
     related to reading. (Illinois Reading Council 1994b, 1)

There is strong convergence between the statements—an assumption
that reading (whatever it is) is a given, a belief in reading as "good," and a
belief in the promotion and expansion of reading and readers in general.
These are the broad values to which members at all levels of the organization can agree.

Charter, Structures, and Activities
The major activity of all levels of the organization is to produce activities
that will benefit the members in their pursuit of these goals. At the local

level these activities are usually short, one-shot professional development events. At the state level, at least in Illinois, it is well accepted that the major purpose of the state organization is to produce the annual state conference, also a professional development opportunity. At the national level, while the annual conference may be the most visible part of organizational work to many members, in truth, it is one of an array of activities that range from publishing, lobbying, and policy work, to the support of research. As state and local councils mature in their approaches, create a more stable and committed membership base, and move away from serving more as a social club, they also expand the array of their activities and the sophistication of their approaches.

The local leadership and its activities are described in depth in the upcoming chapters, however, suffice it to say here that at all levels of the organization there are similar governing offices of president, vice president (also program chair), secretary, and treasurer. Their activities are guided by the charter and bylaws of the organization.

In addition there is a plethora of committees; some reflect the national organization's initiatives and some are the result of state or local initiatives. For instance, across the nation, state councils and their local counterparts will have committees or an individual dedicated to overseeing the annual Honor Council application process or the Newspaper in Education work.

There are two kinds of committees: standing (permanently established) and ad hoc (temporarily established). Honor Council, for instance, is a standing position or committee, while in Illinois, as an example, Adult Literacy is an ad hoc committee. Committees are shifted from ad hoc to standing through a vote of the councils.

Membership, Place, and Solvency

The formal relationships among the parts, particularly in regard to membership, can be initially confusing. When you join a local council, at least in Illinois, you automatically become a member of the state organization.

Membership in IRA is, however, a separate decision. All local officers and state officials are required to be card-carrying IRA members. The state organization itself is an affiliate of IRA. All local and state charters must be approved by IRA.

At the state level, as well as at the national level, there is also a range of special interest groups to which members can pledge membership on top of their IRC or IRA membership.

In 1994, when this study was conducted, IRA directly represented some 93,000 members, 93 percent of whom resided in the United States and

Canada. It owned its own office building in Newark, Delaware, and employed a staff of about ninety. The annual budget of the organization was close to $7.5 million, 50 percent of which was derived from membership dues, 20 percent from the numerous conferences the group sponsors, 20 percent from book sales, 7 to 8 percent from list rentals and advertising, and 2 to 3 percent from royalties and interest (Bob Jones, IRA Director of Finance, interview, June 22, 1993).

When speaking of reading councils within the United States, IRA is only the tip of the iceberg. Of these 93,000 IRA members, about 55,000 were also members of one of the twelve hundred state, provincial and/or local councils in the United States or elsewhere. There were also approximately 200,000 members of local councils who were not IRA members, but through their organization's affiliation with IRA they had some connection to the international group. Theoretically this swells the numbers of the national-international group to close to 300,000 members (Bob Jones, IRA Director of Finance, interview, June 22, 1993).

Of this group of 300,000, 6,620 were members of the Illinois Reading Council (IRC), which was chartered in 1968. IRC members who were members of the IRA numbered 3,932. IRC is one of the largest state councils. Due to the relatively large proportion of IRA members who are also IRC members (over 50 percent), IRC wields considerable influence at the national level, as these IRC-IRA members form a formidable voting block.

IRC is itself composed of a number of smaller councils—twenty-seven local councils and seven special interest councils—the largest of which, the statewide Illinois Whole Language special interest group, has 730 members and the smallest of which, rural Vermillion Valley in eastern Illinois, has 16 members. The thirty-four local and special interest councils are divided into seven regions: six geographical zones and one zone comprising only special interest councils (Illinois Reading Council 1993b).

The seven special interest councils are the Administrators and Reading Special Interest Council (AARSIC), College Instructors of Reading Professionals (CIRP), Early Childhood Special Interest Council (ECSIC), Illinois Council for Affective Reading Education (ICARE), Illinois Whole Language Reading Council (IWL), Secondary Reading League (SRL), and Illinois Chapter 1 Teachers' Association (ICTA). Surprisingly, despite the importance of Chapter 1 in IRA's development, ICTA is the most recently formed special interest group, created during the 1993–94 school year. Many members augment their local-state membership with memberships to one or more special interest councils. There are also members who do not belong to a local council but maintain their state membership through membership in a special interest council.

As mentioned above, the largest council of any sort, special interest or local, is the Illinois Whole Language Reading Council (IWL). This body began twenty years ago as a special interest group with an emphasis on language experience, evolving with the times to the whole language title. They have been a very active and very visible group within IRC. They sponsor an annual conference for professionals as well as the annual Illinois Young Authors conference. They brought the Australian staff development program, "Frameworks," to the states and sponsored training for IRC members. At the 1993 IWL preconference to IRC, IWL distributed two thousand dollars in awards of about one to two hundred dollars to attendees. IWL's high visibility and the rather strong philosophical stance they take within an organization that tends to back away from advocacy positions also mean that they have been the focus of many of the major controversies within the organization.

Although there were no statistics on state membership demographics, I can say with certainty that most members, like reading council members around the country, are white females between the ages of thirty-five and sixty-five. Most are experienced elementary teachers. Many are Chapter 1 teachers. A small but prominent portion of members teach reading methods in public and private state colleges around the state. In Illinois the highest concentration of members is in the northern part of the state, particularly in the suburbs around Chicago. In the central and southern parts of the state, council members also tend to come from the more suburban or rural districts where staff development opportunities are fewer.

The geographical home of IRC is Bloomington, Illinois, where the organization maintains a modest office on the perimeter of town, next door to a veterinarian's office and nearby a busy highway bordered by numerous strip malls. Up to the time of this study, IRC employed only one part-time employee, the incomparable Arlene Pennie, who served as the organization's executive secretary. Pennie managed most day-to-day office needs of the organization, and oversaw membership logistics and conference registration. In 1993 and 94, the organization also began to employ the services of a part-time bookkeeper to assist with their financial needs.

IRC experienced a financial crisis in the early 1990s, and, as a result, the leadership has worked hard since that time to put the organization on a more sensible financial footing. The effort has paid off. As of March 31, 1994, their total assets were $389,347.70 (Illinois Reading Council 1994a).

Because they are a volunteer organization, almost all of the labor to produce council events, publications, etc. is donated. If this labor donation were to be given a dollar amount and counted as a donation to the organization, the group's assets would soar immensely. The same could be said of any part of the reading councils.

Paper Membership: Publications and Promotional Items

Many reading council members participate in part or in full in the organization through the various council publications. This is what I have come to call "paper membership." This continuous stream of paper enters the home monthly. In addition to the newspapers of reading news, and journals on teaching strategies and research, at the national level there is also a full publishing program that includes books, monographs, audiotapes, and videotapes. At each level, promotional items are given away or sold. These range from mugs and T-shirts to posters and bags. They may promote the organization, the general idea of reading, or a specific event or initiative.

IRA Publications

All IRA members receive the organization's monthly newspaper (*Reading Today*). In addition, they may also subscribe to the organization's journals: *The Reading Teacher, Journal of Reading, Reading Research Quarterly,* and *Lectura y Vida.* In addition to the base rate of sales, IRA estimates that for every IRA journal that is sold, there are about twelve Xerox copies produced from it (IRA Publications staff, interview, June 23, 1993).

IRA also publishes numerous monographs and books. These range from practical, teacher-oriented materials to more theoretical and scientific research pieces.

In recent years, the organization has also begun to move in the direction of new media—audio and videotapes, web pages, CDs, and other resources that make use of new technological possibilities.

All members also receive the program for the annual conference; this serves as a regular update on reading topics and concerns.

State and Local Publications

The state organization's newsletter, *The Communicator,* is distributed to members five times a year. In order of space and prominence devoted to these issues, this communication organ *(a)* advertises the state conference, *(b)* maintains the other business functions of the state organization, *(c)* promotes achievements, awards, and recognition programs (either its own, IRA's, or those of outside organizations), *(d)* disseminates information on special interest councils and state level committees, *(e)* acts as a conduit between council audiences and outside enterprises, and *(f)* serves as a tool to leverage IRC's political power within IRA. Interestingly, *The Communicator* provides virtually no space for talk about policy concerns, helpful hints for teachers to use in their classrooms, or information about the work that other councils are doing.

The Communicator is the communication vehicle of that year's IRC president. The president's personal hand-picked assistant, the corresponding secretary, produces the newsletter. Thus, presidents design the newsletter form and content in line with their views of the organization's needs and their hopes for its future directions. While there is change in the format and contents from presidency to presidency, the shift is not wide, and, for the most part, the priorities established above continue.

There is also a state reading journal, *The Illinois Reading Council Journal* (IRCJ), which is published quarterly. It combines descriptive pieces with research studies conducted by university educators in the local colleges.

Although the graphic quality is more sophisticated, the format, tone, and concerns of *The Communicator* are similar in many ways to that of the local council newsletters. Each local issue contains a letter from the president that, like the other articles, is upbeat, positive, and appeals to similar arguments about the value of reading and membership in the organization. Local council newsletters tend to appear sporadically across the school year, often in advance of the next council event. Some resemble simple letters to members with informational flyers inserted. Others look like school newsletters. These are divided into simple columns and illustrated with the sort of clip art that is available in schools.

Conclusions

In opening an IRC state leadership meeting for newly elected local leaders, a state leader told the group: "You are part of a special, magical group of literacy leaders. You belong to one of the largest councils in the US of IRA, a group with other 93,000 members. Many state and national leaders have emerged from this group. Three of the nine members of the [IRA] board this year were from this group. Welcome. Enjoy the day and the year." Through this statement, the state leader enlarged and elevated local members' perspectives of their work, connecting it to the work of the larger organization.

At the same meeting, a representative from IRA elevated the "localness" of reading council work through emphasizing the importance of the grassroots workers and the reliance of the state and national organization on the participation of these members.

> He describes the army structure. There is a squad, the unit, the company, and the division. In his eyes, the squad is the local council executive committee, the platoon is the local council, the company is the state organization, and the division is IRA. . . . He passed on a saying from the army: "The division doesn't exist. The company doesn't exist. But, what's in it for the grunts? . . . The division is only as strong as the company or platoons. . . . It's the grunts. It's you. It's not people in headquarters or professional associates. It's you. . . . How does IRA connect to states. We are one large unit and we have to work together." (Excerpt from field notes)

These two statements, uttered at the same meeting, are symbolic to me of the way the organization views the reflexive relationship among the layers of the pyramid that is the entity known as the reading councils. Cohesion across the layers is maintained through the repetition of structure, goals, and discourse as they emerge in activities and publications. The term "living reading" means, for me, the ways members enact their views about reading in the world and, conversely, how reading becomes a means of describing, defining, positioning, and connecting themselves and their organization to the world and other communities of practice.

Why Reading?

The question, "Why reading?" reaches deep into the historical context of American educational history and, in particular, the gendered nature of that history. The development of reading as a discipline and profession over the last century and a half is closely tied to women's entry into the world of education and civic organizations. It is also closely tied to the development of modern educational publishing.

Women, Education, Civic Organizations, and Reading: A Historical Perspective

Women entered the teaching profession full force midway in the last century. Since colonial times, women had been present as educators in private dame schools, but men dominated teaching positions in the public schools. Women were found in public schools from the 1820s, particularly during the summer sessions, but it was between the 1840s and the 1880s that women gradually came to replace men as teachers. By 1888,

63 percent of all American teachers were women, and this figure reached 90 percent in American cities. Grumet reports, "In 1870, women constituted 60 percent of the nation's teachers; by 1900, 70 percent; by 1910, 80 percent. Figures from the mid-1970's indicate that 67.1 percent of all teachers are women (The percentages in elementary teaching are 87 percent. . .)" (1988, 43). Not surprisingly, though, in 1888 only four percent of female educators held administrative positions (Grumet 1988, 38).

Several forces were at work in the shift from a male to a female teaching force. Changing demographics, economic conditions, and social conditions all played a role. Industrialization, along with immigration, was occurring at a rapid pace in many American cities, at the same time that westward expansion led to the founding of many new communities across the continent. These changes led to new educational concerns—for the education of immigrant children and the establishment of frontier schools. Education came to be seen as a means of bringing young people into the fold, preparing them for work roles, and serving as an antidote against various social evils. Because women teachers were paid only about one-third of what male teachers could expect to be paid, they were an ideal economic resource for the expanding teaching labor market (Grumet 1988, 37).

But the economic reasons for women's entry into the educational labor market did not occur in a vacuum. This entry took place at a time of broad national discussion about women's role in society. Through these debates rose conceptions of the virtuous woman, docile and nurturing, conceptions in which the role of motherhood came to dominate. Women were seen to be innately endowed as mothers to nurture the young, as teachers to instruct the young, and as members of society to redeem the nation through the young. As embodiments of virtue, their duty was to inculcate others with that virtue.

The transformation of public schools from male taught to female taught within the space of a few decades must be attributed in some part to the work of Catherine Beecher, who in 1843 began a national movement to effect this change. Beecher traveled around the country raising funds for the development of schools and the training of teachers. A skilled public speaker, politician, and frequently published writer, she called for a national movement, similar to that of the temperance one, that would enlist Protestant women wholeheartedly in social projects, particularly education. Beecher depicted this role for Protestant women as one parallel to the Catholic nun, making self-denial for the social good a cornerstone of her platform. Women, Beecher believed, held the power to shape good character and, thus, could transform society on many levels—in their homes, communities, and nationally—and their duty was to do so (Sklar 1973). In this, Beecher built from Rousseau's conceptualization of Sophie, as the emotional, character-building half of Emile, but went several steps beyond Rousseau to make Sophie, through the same traits, the active guardian of community and nation (Rousseau 1979). Simplistically put, where men came to be in charge of the production of society, women became exclusively responsible for the reproduction of society (Martin 1985).

Parallel to women's entry in large numbers into the labor force as teachers, women were also evolving new civic roles for themselves through the development of social clubs and other civic organizations. Historian Scott states, "About the middle of the 1790's what would in time become a vast and all-pervasive social movement began to take shape as American women of all ages began to form voluntary associations" (1984, 261). The early women's benevolent associations, like their later forms, shared certain characteristics: "(1) It was an all-woman group. (2) The women were seeking to educate themselves. (3) The leader was a woman of unusually powerful personal qualities. (4) The substance was religious. (5) The original purpose widened as time went by" (Scott 1984, 262). Scott also found that these benevolent groups organized themselves in highly similar ways. None were without a charter; each had rules about how the meetings should be conducted and how the money would be used (Scott 1992, 13).

Writing of a later period, feminist Charlotte Gilman stated, "The whole country is budding into women's clubs. The clubs are uniting and federating by towns, states, nations" (qtd. in Rothman 1978, 65). For example, in 1892, the General Federation of Women's Clubs formed with 495 affiliates and over 100,000 members. By 1890, the Women's Christian Temperance Union, founded in 1873, had 160,000 members in chapters across the nation (Rothman 1978). These benevolent associations developed working girls' clubs and rescue missions and organized investigations of social organizations charged with the care of the young, the poor, the infirm, and the antisocial.

The Protestant roots of this activity must be acknowledged. Beecher's drive to expand women's roles in public education appealed directly to Protestant beliefs and social practices. As such, it hypothesized a public school system that was in effect a Protestant school system. But the foundation for Beecher's work had been planted before her time. The movement to develop women's intellectual and reforming social groups built upon the branches of the women's benevolent and missionary societies that flourished in the early 1800s in most local Protestant churches. These groups were the roots from which the larger national organizations and visions later grew. The term "Protestant Nun" came from the work of the Women's Christian Temperance Union, a virtually all-Protestant organization. It came to encompass a picture of woman as a socially reforming creature who plied her trade within and across these various women's civic groups.

The role of reading as a force in women's civic organizations in the 1800s must also be acknowledged. Some of the earliest women's social organizations were reading clubs, where women got together to read and discuss a book. These clubs served many purposes: a place to maintain the intellectual skills for which one had attended college, a place to get an education, a mutual improvement society, or an extension of the intimate college clubs that educated women had experienced (Rothman 1978, 65). For many, as Long reports, reading clubs were the first step to collectivity, voice, and action. "Very quickly their study circles began addressing more public (although still appropriately womanly) issues of progressive reform: pure food and drug laws, protective legislation for women and children and the establishment of public schools and libraries, parks, and healthy water supplies" (Long 1993, 195). Women's reading clubs continue to thrive and flourish today. And, in an ironic, self-reflexive twist, members within organizations like the International Reading Association and the National Council of Teachers of English have recently begun to build reading clubs for teachers in schools across the country returning women's reading clubs to the field of reading professionals (Hansen 1993, 35).

In summary, the reading councils we see today have roots that reach deep into American educational and social history. They are predominantly composed of women who teach the elementary grades, a circumstance related to the changes in education that occurred in the mid-1880s. In form, practice, and outlook they build directly upon the great tradition of women's civic organizations, also a phenomenon of the middle to late 1800s. Not surprisingly, in the structure of their leadership and programs there are many parallels to historical and contemporary civic groups. The substance of their concerns—reading and its instruction—is closely related to the discussion of women's roles as educational nurturers, roles that proceeded from that period. These groups are also linked to the powerful role that reading groups played in the development of women's own form of power as community leaders. Finally, they are saturated with Protestant overtones. As this brief historical overview indicates, the influence of Protestantism in a Protestant culture cannot be confined to church attendance alone, as it includes all manner of other affairs, participation in groups across the community, not to mention the development of one's beliefs and identity. These practices are interlinked and mutually reflexive.

Reading: Discipline and Profession

In beginning a discussion of reading in our culture with a discussion of women's roles in this field, I take an unorthodox position. Most histories of reading begin with discussion of the materials by which reading was taught, expanding from there to consideration of a generic "teacher" and "instructional techniques." Women's issues figure almost not at all in the broad discussions of the shifts in theories, instructional ideas, and the development of materials. And yet it is clear that the field of reading, as it developed from the 1800s and through the twentieth century up to this very day, is a highly gendered proposition.

Feminist curriculum theorist Madeline Grumet argues that today's schools, much as schools in the 1820s, portray a complex and conflicted relationship between patriarchal power and matriarchal frustration. Men are seen as producers who live in worlds where time is contractual and defined, and they oversee women whose work is seen as reproductive, fulfilling maintenance, not creative needs, and whose time is viewed as unbounded. Women were (and are) "expected to be the medium through which the laws, rules, language and order of the father, the principal, the employer were communicated to the child" (Grumet 1988, 84). Grumet argues that women are complicit in this process, reproducing in their classrooms the isolation of the home. Their attempts at resistance are often ineffectual, as they seek emotional support from others rather than taking political action or refuse to nurture themselves as they allow themselves to be overwhelmed by others' endless demands on their time.

Gendered as the history of reading is, that history has been until recently curiously silent about the ways that reading, work, and identity are constructed as gendered topics.

Reading: Multiple Meanings

Definitions of reading shift fluidly throughout the history of the last two centuries, as they assimilate new meanings and functions. In colonial times, the object of reading education was instrumental, closely tied to moral education and the development of commercial skills. Throughout the 1800s the object of instruction was aimed at oral reading or elocution. At various times, reading has meant the study of "the classics." In the last few decades, reading has come to mean the comprehension process (Monaghan and Saul 1987).

Each of these various goals implies considerations regarding curriculum, materials, and instructional techniques. So for instance, the early McGuffy readers (a reading textbook that first appeared in 1836 and was available in various editions for close to a century) stressed moral stories and object lessons; their passages tended to be relatively short, appropriate for oral reading. In later readers, literature content increased, as did the length of passages, also a consequence of the shift in emphasis from oral to silent reading. Teachers' manuals for basal reading series produced in the 1980s are thick with information on how to teach comprehension and related skills. The beliefs about what is important in reading and, thus, how one should teach it and with what materials have never been separate from discussions of the larger social questions: what is it that we want for our society? How must we educate children to meet those goals? (Graff 1991; Kaestle et al. 1991; Venezky, 1986).

Not surprisingly, theories about the meaning of literacy, theories which try to explain the differences in approaches, abound. Autonomous theories of literacy portray it as a technological tool of rational people, implying that a huge divide exists between the literate and the nonliterate (Ong 1982). Those who take an ideological perspective see literacy as something constructed through social interaction. An ideological outlook is deeply concerned with the power relations that are part of literacy practices and the ways that literacy constructs differences of class, race, ethnicity, or gender (Street 1993). Drawing upon post-modern critiques, critical theories consider literacy "as so many discourses which in inscribing meaning are crucially involved in the formation of human subjects" (Lankshear and McLaren 1993, 10). A highly influential view is Louise Rosenblatt's transactional model of reading, a model that I will discuss at greater length later in this chapter. Rosenblatt's work fits within the larger tradition of reader-response theory developed within the framework of literary criticism (Connell 1994; Rosenblatt 1978). Theorizing about literacy or reading is an important aspect of the evolution of reading practices themselves, sometimes reflecting what has been and sometimes driving what could be.

The Scientific Study of Reading
The modern study of reading as we know it could be said to begin with Edward Lee Thorndike's experimental work in the early 1900s and the

development of educational psychology. Thorndike "believed in the possibility of establishing education as a science, and was convinced that quantitative measurement was the most powerful tool at his disposal" (Monaghan and Saul, 1987, 96). The principles that Thorndike established were continued through the work of his two students, William S. Gray and Arthur Gates. William S. Gray, the first president of IRA and ostensibly the most famous reading researcher of his era, taught at the University of Chicago; Arthur Gates taught at Columbia Teacher's College, as did Thorndike. Both men were prolific authors, publishing innumerable reading research studies. They trained many students in the virtues of the scientific approach to reading.

The belief in a science of education fit neatly with the then contemporary economic and social discourses of progressivism calling for a brave new world run on the efficient principles of business aided by science. This philosophy, as translated to education, sought to eliminate waste in curriculum and instruction, emphasizing functional uses of language and measurement techniques as a means of achieving these goals (Shannon 1989). "The belief in science was also part of a belief in professionalism. The faith in a science of schooling was part of a discourse related to the professionalization occurring in the social and economic structures of American society. The Progressive Era is one manifestation of a larger change in the social organization of work and the commodification of knowledge through the formation of structured communities of experts" (Popkewitz 1987, 10).

In tandem with these conditions, the field, or profession, of reading grew steadily during the 1930s and 1940s. Whereas in 1930 there were no university classes offered on the topic (Squire 1991) during the following two decades a number of university centers of study and teacher training programs were developed. Reading specialists begin to be seen in schools, and states developed reading certification requirements (Ruth 1991). This expanding crop of reading experts found ready employment in the basal reading industry, which was developing and expanding during these years, and many of the most famous names in reading research were also authors of the major reading series. William S. Gray headed the best-selling textbook series known to most of us as "Dick and Jane," that is, the Curriculum Foundation series published by Scott Foresman and Company (Luke 1988). Unlike earlier series, which mixed various literary genre, moral tales with fables and snippets from classics, this new series contained: "lexically, syntactically and semantically controlled texts about modern inter- and post-war life in an industrial democracy. These tales were fabricated solely for the purposes of teaching the 'skills' and 'habits' of reading. The application of scientific theories of reading and linguistic development to the engineering of basal readers completed the shift from traditional literary content" (Luke 1988, 71).

The basal reading textbook, based upon principles of the science of education, has reigned virtually supreme up until the present time. It stands as *the* reading program in 90 percent of American classrooms (Shannon 1989), and it represents the largest share of educational text-book spending (Chall and Squire 1991).

This is not to say that there have not been opposing voices to this state of affairs. In 1938, Louise Rosenblatt's *Literature as Exploration* put forth the reader-response position, which offered new perspectives on the reading process. Following in the footsteps of the educational experiments of Francis Parker, John Dewey, and others, there has also been an alternative literacy movement to the basal-driven classroom (Shannon 1989, 1990). None of these, however, ever reached the strength and breadth of the position held by the basal reader and the scientific approach to reading embedded in its form and content.

Monaghan and Saul (1987) credit a number of factors as conducive to the development of reading as a profession, factors that led eventually to the formation of the International Reading Association. These include the existence of a substantial body of research on reading, legitimating it as a discipline, and the presence of reading luminaries such as Gray and Gates. The work of leading reading researchers, and their name recognition, was closely connected to reading basal programs that were used across the United States and in many other countries, through business creating a researcher-practitioner link that existed in few other educational fields.

Organizing the Field

The National Council of Teachers of English (NCTE) was founded in 1911, initially as a means of protesting the domination of the high school English curriculum by the literary canon of college entrance exams. Thus, from its beginnings, NCTE never adequately included elementary teachers' concerns regarding the English curriculum. And in the first several decades of its existence, as interest in reading as a field grew, it also failed to address this contingent. Many educators interested in reading were also concerned with reading failure or disability, and they, too, felt that NCTE did not meet their needs.

These three major constituents—reading teachers and researchers, teachers and researchers concerned with educational disabilities, and elementary teachers—began to pull away from NCTE in the late 1940s. In 1947, the National Association of Remedial Teachers (NART) was formed, followed by the formation, in 1948, of the International Council for the Improvement of Reading Instruction (ICIRI). NART and ICIRI merged to become the International Reading Association (IRA) in 1955 (Jerrolds 1977).

From its inception, then, IRA's reading agenda has been strongly influenced by concerns with reading failure and experimental research in reading. "The metaphor of disablement (if not of disease) that was inherent in the organization of the parent bodies of the International Reading Association is one that is crucial to an understanding of the profession" (Monaghan and Saul, 1987, 105).

For the reasons described above, IRA was strongly positioned to grow and thrive, and two fortuitous historical incidents promoted its agenda even further. First, in 1955 Rudolph Flesch published *Why Johnny Can't Read,* a polemical call to arms against the whole-word method of reading and a battle cry for the phonics approach. Extremely popular, *Why Johnny Can't Read* held its own on the best-seller list for many weeks, selling numerous copies, and, as a consequence, introduced many Americans to the concept of reading as a critical and foundational skill as well as to the debates about reading surrounding reading instruction. Although many IRA members had strong critiques of the phonics program proposed by Flesch, they benefitted from the publicity he brought to reading issues (Ruth 1991).

The second critical incident in the early history of IRA was the passage, in 1965, of the Elementary and Secondary Education Act (ESEA) that provided over one billion dollars for the education of disadvantaged children. Title I, later Chapter 1, was developed from the premise that reading was the foundational skill that children from disadvantaged circumstances had to master if they were to break out of the cycle of poverty. Tied to this belief was the notion that "society had an illness and needed specialists to make it well again" (Monaghan and Saul, 1987, 109). Funds for this program had to "supplement, not supplant" classroom services and, thus, could be used to hire reading specialists, not classroom teachers. In addition to the financial support for staff, districts also received generous awards for materials and staff development. Teachers and supervisors in this program were a natural membership pool for the growing IRA organization, which developed a special conference strand just to meet their needs. Legislative issues related to Chapter 1 figure very importantly on IRA's agenda. For many years the organization has employed a lobbyist on Capitol Hill whose duty is to keep track of these concerns.

The cause of education, in general, and English/language arts, specifically, was also bolstered by infusions of federal money for research, development, and dissemination projects on a scale heretofore unknown. In the early 1960s, Project English provided support for over fifty basic research projects, demonstration centers, and a series of semi-annual conferences. In 1964, the National Defense Education Act (NDEA) of 1958 was expanded to include support for "English, reading, and the teaching of English to second language speakers" (Ruth 1991, 90). In 1966, the U.S. Office of Education established fourteen demonstration centers and twenty laboratory facilities devoted to educational issues (Ruth 1991). Each of these acts contributed to the widening national interest in reading and the belief that reading should be a crucial national concern.

NCTE and IRA differ significantly in relationship to their activity in the policy realm. NCTE has been far more active in developing policy positions and engaging with other organizations to pursue policy concerns. IRA, on the other hand, has translated its appropriate political role as one of informant, not agitator. Ruth quotes a personal communication from Alan Farstrup, then IRA research director and now the organization's executive director, on this issue:

> There are many widely varying points of view and philosophies represented within the Association. I view the Association as a forum for the competition and clarification of these ideas and philosophies rather than as an institution whose job it is to advocate specific points of view unless there is a strong consensus across the entire membership with regard to particular issues. Certainly when the question revolves around matters of basic literacy and the importance of literacy we can all agree on the correct stance to adopt. When the issues revolve around contrasting, underlying philosophies of education—for example whether we should insist on highly structured teacher directed lessons or whether we should follow an approach where the teacher is not as directive—then the Association's role as an open forum becomes very important. (1991, 102)

I heard much the same in my interviews and conversations with IRC and IRA members at all levels of the organization, that is, the belief that they are a highly diverse collection of interests and yet have a common core of understanding to which all can agree. Also embedded in this statement is the belief that it is not the role of a professional organization to tell people what to do, but rather to inform others of the possibilities through the maintenance of an open, free, competitive marketplace of ideas. Indeed, for all the talk about diversity of ideas, there is remarkable consensus among members on these principles.

The Shifting Sands of Reading: From Comprehension to Whole Language

In 1976, the federal government awarded a grant to the University of Illinois for the establishment of the Center for the Study of Reading. For fifteen years the center churned out research, technical reports, books, and other products on reading research. The many hundreds of technical reports, with their distinctive goldenrod covers, can be found in almost every university library and are familiar to most university students who have taken a course in reading. Publications issuing from the center, like *Becoming a Nation of Readers* (Anderson et al. 1985) or *Beginning to Read: Thinking and Learning about Print* (Adams 1990), are now classical references. The researchers, staff members, and graduate students (later to be researchers in their own right) associated with the Center for the Study of Reading have been prominent in the field. Important names associated with the center include: Richard C. Anderson, P. David Pearson, Jean Osborn, Jana Mason, Bertram Bruce, William Nagy, Delores Durkin, and Taffy Raphael, to name only a few.

The center's distinctive contribution to reading was the attention it paid to what cognitive psychology could say about the field of reading and, building from that theoretical background, the development of a comprehension focus to the notion of reading. Comprehension became the focus of reading interest in the late 1970s and 1980s, thanks to the work of the Center for the Study of Reading. This is an interactive theory of reading, one which emphasizes the meaning-making process of the act and takes account of the prior knowledge that readers bring to their work and the ways that this will affect their reading. It draws heavily on schema theory and the insights of developmental psychology. The emphasis on comprehension promoted by the Center helped to shift educators' attention away from the scientific reading agenda with its emphasis on isolated skills and toward a greater interest in the processes of reading.

The center has enjoyed a long and close relationship with IRA. Center staff have been frequent presenters at IRA conferences and state reading conferences. They established a one-day preconference research program, featuring, for the most part, center staff presenting their research idea; and this research program became an expected part of IRA conferences. P. David Pearson, former associate director of the center, served on the IRA national board of directors and Richard Anderson, Delores Durkin, and P. David Pearson are recipients of one of IRA's highest awards for service to the profession, the William S. Gray citation of merit. P. David Pearson and Richard Anderson are also members of IRA's Reading Hall of Fame (IRA Desktop Reference 1992).

The Center for the Study of Reading was one part, and a very prominent part, of a shifting trend in the field away from the earlier scientific approach to reading. Other notable voices include Frank Smith and his work on psycholinguistics (1978) and Kenneth Goodman, whose name, at that time, was synonymous with psycholinguistics and miscue analysis (Bergeron 1990). Goodman served as president of IRA during 1981 and 1982. His wife, Yetta, also a prominent voice in the field, has more recently served as a member of the IRA Board of Directors.

The Rise of Whole Language

Goodman is a critical link in the evolution from the cognitive-comprehension focus on reading to the current interest in whole language. In the last several years, the discourse of whole language has become so persuasive in the educational world that there are few members of IRA who do not now subscribe to it in some way. Even those who express some disenchantment toward it (either as a philosophical or political movement), such as the proponents of the balanced reading movement within IRA, position their arguments in reference to it. Members I interviewed believed that "we're all moving toward whole language."

Whole language goes beyond the interactive perspective, which I would ascribe as the cognitive-comprehension positions, to embrace a transactive view of reading, a term drawn from Louise Rosenblatt's Deweyan-based reader-response theory. According to Goodman;

> Reading is a constructive process: both the text and its meaning are constructed by the reader. That means that at any point in time there are two or more texts during reading: the published text and the reader's text. In the transactions, both the reader and the text are changed. The reader's knowledge and schemata are changed, and the text is changed as the reader constructs it to fit expectations and world knowledge. In this emerging consensus, what the reader brings to the text is as important as anything in the text. Comprehension always depends on the readers' knowledge, beliefs, schemata, and language ability. (Goodman 1992, 358)

Whole language advocates see their stance as philosophical, pedagogical, and political. As a paradigmatic shift, it requires the repositioning of all parties from teachers, students, administrators, and parents to publishers, policy makers, researchers, and national literacy organizations. One of its central planks is the demand for teacher empowerment and an acknowledgment of teachers' work as a locus for knowledge creation. As a consequence, whole language advocates have been in the forefront of recent opposition to the basal reader technology. "[I]t directly contradicts certain power arrangements. For instance, whole language tries to get rid of the stranglehold basal technology has on teachers and kids. Whole language criticisms of the basal reader technology imply that teachers should abandon that technology, not just substitute a different material, i.e. literature, but take control of how and what to teach. Advocating the abandonment of basal readers attacks the control that publishers have over both the tests and the curriculum . . . that's pretty political" (Edelsky 1992, 325–326).

Reading councils today are composed of members whose beliefs encompass the gamut of the spectrum, from scientific reading perspectives and an emphasis on comprehension to whole language and related psycho- and sociolinguistic perspectives. These approaches exist sometimes more and sometimes less compatibly.

Publishers and Reading Councils

Reading council practice is closely linked to the interests of the communications industry, in particular, to textbook and juvenile trade book publications. Since books are the stuff of reading, the needs and concerns of publishers and reading specialists cannot help but be closely connected. Indeed, in council practice, signs of these connections are visible at every level of the organization. In this section, I describe the ways publishers are related to the development of reading as a discipline and profession and, thus, to the rise of IRA.

As mentioned earlier, the rise of interest in scientific reading instruction in the twentieth century was coupled with the rise in status of reading experts and the development of the basal reading series, based upon a scientific approach to reading promoted by reading experts. As a consequence, basal reading textbooks have dominated reading instruction in the United States since the 1940s (Shannon 1989). This large industry brings in a tidy profit. "Of roughly $1 billion expended by elementary schools on textbooks and related materials in 1986, some 43.6 percent was spent on reading materials . . . Indeed, reading and language arts, when combined with spelling and literature, account for about 60 percent of the instructional dollars . . . And these totals do not include expenditures for library books, newspapers, and other materials directly associated with reading instruction" (Chall and Squire 1991, 121).

Over the last several years, this industry has undergone great changes as mergers and takeovers have completely changed the face of publishing. Where once there were numerous companies competing to get their basal readers into school districts across the country, now there are a handful. "By 1990, there were six corporations that controlled 90 percent of the market: MacMillan/McGraw-Hill (which owns Merrill, SRA, and Barnell Loft), Harcourt, Brace, Jovanovich (which owns Holt, Rinehart), Silver Burdett-Ginn (which bares its merger in its title), Houghton Mifflin, Scott Foresman, and D.C. Heath" (Shannon 1994, 208).

These megafirms now span numerous communications operations, including not only textbook production and the major norm-referenced tests, but also adult and juvenile trade books, computer products of various sorts, media productions, and other aspects of the communication industry. For instance, at the 1994 Toronto IRA conference, the Paramount exhibit space, one of the largest in the hall, displayed banners advertising booths for these firms: Silver Burdett-Ginn, Prentice-Hall, Computer Curriculum Corporation, Modern Curriculum Press, Fearon Teacher Aids, Allyn and Bacon, and Silver Burdett Press. (As you can see, Silver Burdett-Ginn has traded hands since Shannon's 1990 figures.) We have not even begun to comprehend what the possible editorial consequences might be, given the homogenization of ownership in communications.

Economics and cost-effectiveness were not the only forces driving the educational publishing industry over the last decade. School textbook and juvenile trade book publishers have also been rocked by a challenge originating from educators, and that is the whole language movement. As mentioned earlier, whole language is a reference point for most discussions in the reading councils today, and "We are all moving toward whole language" is a constant rallying cry across the reading councils. For publishers, the move to whole language has meant an increased demand for juvenile trade books and closer scrutiny of basal reading series, their premises, content, and form. In some cases, this movement has meant a militant backlash against the basal reading text. For instance, in the IRA newspaper, *Reading Today,* children's book author Mem Fox had this to say about basals: "As teachers we must stop being polite. We must demand all sorts of books written for children . . . and we must demand millions of them. I believe basals are the single greatest cause of illiteracy . . . I believe if basals were banned tomorrow, illiteracy would be wiped out in one generation . . . We must trust ourselves to analyze what we like in books and to use real books with our students . . . What is a real book? Put yourself in the writer's head . . . if the book is written to please rather than to teach, then it's a real book." Fox earned a standing ovation for her provocative comments" (June/July, 1993).

The whole language movement is an umbrella term that encompasses not only a greater interest in juvenile fiction, but also such concerns as writing processes and their connection to reading, and the development of more holistic measures, dubbed "authentic assessment," for understanding students' reading and writing achievement. Indeed, the concerns of the whole language movement touch upon the total range of product topics for the teaching of language arts—reading, literature, spelling, grammar, and composition.

The publishing industry responded to this philosophical shift in various ways. Since many of the megafirms now own both textbook and trade book concerns, they are actually well-positioned to make the most of both markets. They added more contemporary literature selections, modified the methods advocated in the teachers' manuals, created new materials to teach composition, and added portfolio assessment packages. In some cases, they even split up the mammoth reading text into numerous small paperbacks that give the semblance of "real" books. Trade book publishers began to market their books more aggressively to classroom teachers and to package their wares in different ways. In the process of making these responses, publishers assumed more and more of the language of the whole language movement, reflecting these interests in their promotional materials, their presentations to educators, and in the teachers' manuals of the textbooks.

But this talk may be deceptive. At the 1994 annual IRA conference in Toronto, Patrick Shannon and several colleagues made a follow-up presentation to their 1987 basal reading report card (Shannon et al. 1994). Their findings were dampening. They discovered that the scientific approach to reading, as a transmissionist model that divides knowledge into small transferable modules, is still alive and well in the basal reading series, despite attempts to modify it to fit a different paradigm. They found that basals continue to support the status quo in subtle and not so subtle ways, and they raised important concerns about the ability of basals, entrenched as they are within an industry committed to profit as the bottom line, to truly address the philosophical concerns of the whole language movement and its implied educational and social critique.

While there is strong and growing interest in whole language among the reading council ranks, the concept is most closely identified with a newly emerging literacy organization, the Whole Language Umbrella.

The reading councils have had a long, close relationship with the communications industry. The nature of this relationship is, however, hotly disputed and is an awkward topic for many members. Publishing firms and their authors play an important role in the work of the reading councils at all levels. Many of the most important figures in IRA leadership have been well-known consultants and writers for basal reading series. These have included William S. Gray, Arthur Gates, Emmett Betts, David Russell, Guy Bond, Albert J. Harris, Russell Stauffer, and P. David Pearson, to name just a few (Shannon 1989, 29).

The influence of publishing companies makes itself felt throughout the organization in other ways as well, from support for speakers to the presence of exhibit halls. In the following chapters I explore the links between councils and commercial firms in greater depth as I look at the details of their relationship at the level of local practice.

IRA leadership vehemently denies that they are "in the hip pocket of McGraw-Hill or the other major publishers" (IRA staff member, personal communication, June 1993). They resent criticism of the relationship they have with publishers and the support they receive from them. Staff happily retell stories of one-time critics who, once they became more familiar with IRA, realized that IRA was not "the mouthpiece of reading series" and that IRA was not "pushing for one particular series."

On the one hand, staff are quick to say that they are not controlled by publishers, but on the other hand, they are equally quick to admit that without the publishers and other exhibitors the organization, and, in particular, its conferences, would not exist as members now know them. They defend their integrity and intellectual independence, but they also admit that they pay for very few of the speakers who bring them the new ideas they seek—these speakers come at the sponsorship of publishing or other firms.

The relationship among reading councils and publishers is a complex and multifaceted one. Understanding it is complicated by members' uncomfortableness with many aspects of the subject. The communications industry intertwines with reading teachers' practice—in the classroom and as council members. The significance of its products and the role these products play in shaping ideas about reading, particularly the value of textbooks, should not be underestimated:

> . . . The textbooks a school, a district, or a state approves or uses are often the *only* symbols of what schools at large do.
>   . . . publishers propose while the regulators dispose. . . The effect of this structure has been to give enormous responsibility and enormous problems to the publishing industry: it must define the nature of the curriculum, both as a fact and a symbol, and develop appropriate materials to support that curriculum
>   . . . the *marketplace* represented by the school *system* is necessarily the major force influencing what the textbook publishing industry develops in its role as the principal national curriculum development agent, and how development is

undertaken. The way the industry sees that market determines the practices of the industry. (Westbury 1990, 2, 8, 11)

For publishers, the membership of the reading councils and the numerous events they sponsor are important nodes of the "marketplace represented by the school system."

Conclusions

The next several chapters detail what it means to "live reading." These chapters describe the minutiae of council life, from the organization and activities of local councils to the hopes and aspirations of members. My goal is to provide a picture of council life that will be recognizable to insiders and outsiders. I aim to acknowledge both the convergence and divergence of perspectives that council members bring, the complexity of the organization as it is positioned on the contemporary educational scene, and the contradictions that arise in the course of that positioning.

Note

1   I refer throughout the text to the International Reading Association as a national organization because the vast majority of its members are located within the continental United States and the organization itself is built in response to fundamentally American educational issues and concerns. While IRA does much to promote its international image and projects, it would be a misnomer to construe it as an international organization in the same sense as an organization like CARE or Amnesty International. I know that this position will not endear me to many IRA leaders, but after long thought I believe it is the fairest depiction.

Part II

LOCAL COUNCIL MEMBERS AND LOCAL COUNCIL PRACTICE

Chapter 4

Knitting across Practice: Planning the Council Year

The local reading councils are the focus of my study, in particular, the four councils and the membership of the Raven River, Boxwood, Illinois Heights, and Prairie Councils. The volunteer work of council members nests among many demands: their daily work in schools, school administration, or community organizations; the demands of their families and friends; and the numerous other worthy community projects that demand their attention.

Like the membership, the organization, too, exists in a betwixt and between location. It depends upon the goodwill of the volunteers who plan and attend. events; the support of local school districts and businesses to provide meeting space and refreshments and to urge local educators and others to participate in council events; and the largesse of publishing companies to provide speakers, the draw of exhibits, and support for various other council needs.

Because it is a volunteer organization, membership in the councils is in constant flux. Members cycle into the councils at different physical locations, move through the organization on different trajectories, and cycle out at various points in their careers as volunteers. Some will never enter deeply into the intricacies of council life, while others will be consumed by reading council activities for many years.

Learning about the organization is a process that unfolds over time as members participate in organizational activities. The knowledge of what the local councils are is embedded in the planning and execution of council events and the stories that members share about past events. The execution of these activities draws widely upon members' shared knowledge about the schools and communities in which they reside.

Local groups may change considerably from year to year in their approaches to planning, their ambiance, and their concerns, as new members introduce different approaches. However, there is also much that stays the same. These existing structures and norms shape new members' perspectives in directions that fit with the traditional ethos of councils.

The process by which council members create the council year reminds me much of knitting, putting me in mind of a large multicolored sweater in which the knitter must draw in various contrasting yarns across the back for the pattern to emerge. Eventually I came to label this process "knitting across practice." In this chapter, I employ a variation of this knitting myself. Field notes from a local council planning meeting represent my base color. To this base I add various strands of explanation about the councils and their work. In this way, I hope to provide a cogent description of the structure of local councils and the forms of participation, and an understanding of the norms that guide the shaping of the council year.

Planning the Year: Boxwood Council

It's a lovely spring afternoon in a suburban neighborhood of neatly kept ranch style homes clustered around numerous streets that end in cul-de-sacs. There are seven of us sitting around a dining-room table in the home of Janet Fenner. These women represent the core of Boxwood Reading Council's leadership: Kathy, the current president; Valerie, the past president; Mary, the membership chair; Karen, the recording secretary and also a past president; Janet, the vice president; and Connie, the new assistant to the membership chair. All six are teachers—female and white. They have come to the meeting straight from their classrooms, and although they joke, make small talk, and share a snack as they arrive, they are eager to get down to work so that they can return home to make dinner, or, as in the case of one member, attend the meeting of yet another civic group.

Local Council Structure

At the local level, a board of officers, generally a president, vice president, past president, recording secretary, and treasurer form the nucleus of the leadership group. In many councils, the vice president handles programming, then takes over the presidency the next year, and serves as past president the following year. This makes for a three-year presidential commitment in most local councils.

Committee chairs assist the local board members, often attending board meetings. Some of these positions are required by the state or national structure, and these chairs serve as the local group's liaison to a similar state committee. These positions include such committees as membership, publicity, government and legislation, or parents and reading. Other committees or board positions are idiosyncratic to that particular local group. These might include a liaison to a local adult literacy program, the chair of an annual community service project sponsored by the local group, or a hospitality chair. The local leadership group may be a handful of people who meet irregularly as the need arises at a nearby restaurant or a board of twenty or more persons who have regular monthly meetings and work on activities that can be scheduled as far as two or three years into the future.

Boxwood Council . . .

They consider the upcoming annual statewide leadership meeting—who will be able to go, and how they will share the driving. Then they turn to the major topic of the meeting—planning the council events for the next year. In the past, as members recall, they have had events in September, October, January, February, and April.

"I want a black author, for the upper grades," states Valerie.

"What about Patricia McKissup?"

"I wonder if she's expensive."

Kathy explains that her principal, who is a board member for the local arts council, may be able to assist them to get a grant to bring an expensive author like McKissup. Valerie tells a story about the way IRC member Scott McDonald negotiated a storyteller for them several years ago. McDonald is an active member of the state organization and, because of the special contacts he possesses as one of the higher profile members, often serves as a broker for local councils seeking speakers or other presenters.[1]

This story trips another thought. "Is the state closing out the Educational Service centers?" Karen asks.

"It's up in the air. We've still got a literacy grant into them," answers Valerie.

"Sandy Smith is someone we could also network with for a black author," says Mary, mentioning the name of another IRC leader.

"What about dates for the mall?" Janet asks, shifting discussion to the winter "Read-in at the Mall."

"Who will be chair?"

"We want the frats from Francis College to help unload the materials. We're getting older," Valerie explains.

Karen suggests a local member who works with a program for at-risk adolescents as a possible speaker for another presentation.

The Programs They Plan

The purpose of the local leadership group is to plan programs for their membership and represent that membership to IRC and IRA. For each local group, the annual calendar unfolds in an episodic, but predictable, fashion. "We have our traditions to maintain," explained one member. Most councils produce between four and six public events each year. The range of events is varied, but well-defined. From the four groups I observed, the following events are typical of those presented at the local level.

Expert Presentations

These are by far, the most familiar sort of local event. The presentation is made by an experienced teacher, college instructor, or other expert (state department official, librarian, etc.) on a topic of interest to members. Most talks are between forty-five and sixty minutes. They are highly practical (geared to teachers' concerns) and generally humorous and inspiring. Council members are the primary audience for these events. The expert presentation may be combined with a dinner banquet or box supper. A "Bring Your Administrator" dinner, with an expert presentation, is a popular event among many councils. (The expert presentation will be explored in much greater depth in a later chapter.)

Author Talks

These are presentations made by an author about his or her work. Talks may include discussion of how the author began writing, influences on that writing, how the author identified his or her topic, and the process that the author follows when writing. The talk may also give advice on common pitfalls that writers should avoid. Like the expert presentation, the emphasis is positive, inspiring, and acknowledges teachers' importance to the teaching of reading. The author often tells anecdotes about the publication process, shows his or her books, and, invariably, is available after the presentation to autograph copies of those books, which can be purchased on the spot. The author talk is frequently combined with a meal event, such as a brunch. Members are usually encouraged to bring children to author talks—either their own or members of their class. In conjunction with the author talk, the council may work with local districts to schedule the author to make presentations for school children as well as with publishers, to garner the services of the author and to provide "for sale" copies of their books at the event.

Reading Carnivals or Fairs

This event includes a combination of games, displays, and dramatic presentations. The ones I observed were held in shopping malls; one was held in a school cafeteria. The game segment can include face painting, book walks (like a cake walk but with books for prizes), and other carnival-like games adapted to a book theme. There will often be displays of children's schoolwork, most often related to English instruction, such as child-produced books and children's responses to literature—puppets they have made, shadow boxes, mobiles, etc.—but there may also be products from other curricular areas. In addition, there may be displays from librar-ies and other community groups, such as an adult literacy program, a children's museum, or a tutoring program. Finally, there will be a range of dramatic presentations including read-aloud sessions, storytelling, pup-pet plays, singers, and choral readings. Children's literature may be fur-ther dramatized by council members or others dressed as characters from those stories. These live story characters may wander casually among the carnival goers in much the way that Disney characters wander through Disneyland. They are often used for read-aloud sessions, reading stories of the character they represent. Reading carnivals are open to the com-munity, and families are encouraged to attend.

Make-It and Take-It Workshops
Of the four councils I studied, only one conducted a "Make-it and Take-it Workshop," where teachers lead sessions in which they present success-ful hands-on ideas from their own classroom practice. These workshops often include opportunities to make a classroom resource—a reading game, organizational aid, or other material—to use in one's classroom. Again, this is an event for members, primarily teachers. From my talks with members, it appears that this had been a highly popular offering in earlier years.

Awards Banquet
Only one council I studied held a separate awards banquet at which offic-ers were invested and special awards were distributed. Many councils com-bine this event with another event.

Reading Conference
Local councils and special interest councils may offer their own confer-ences, in addition to the annual statewide conference. One of the local councils I studied offered an annual day-long conference, in conjunction with local schools and the Educational Service District that drew over four hundred participants from the nearby area. A well-known former teacher, now an educational consultant at the state level, was the keynote speaker;

local teachers were featured presenters in the numerous smaller sessions. The statewide Whole Language Special Interest Council produces an annual conference of several days' duration that features national speakers.

Community Service

Community service can come in several forms, from the distribution of awards, plaques, or money to community literacy projects, to actual service donated by members, or to specific literacy projects. Among the groups I studied, awards were given to teachers for curriculum development and for the development of reading collections at homeless shelters, and to an adult literacy program to develop family literacy training. One council engaged in an annual "Book Shower" project that involved soliciting book and/or cash donations from individuals, businesses, and civic organizations for the purchase of books to be given as Christmas presents to families in need. Another council spent considerable time and effort developing and presenting a workshop package for training parents to more effectively promote their children's reading development.

In summary, the expert presentation and the author talk are by far the most common forms of local programming. Reading carnivals, in various forms, are also popular. Make-it and take-it workshops and awards ceremonies are much less so. Information about these events is distributed primarily through the local council newsletter, often as an inserted flyer.

Surprisingly, I did not find member discussion groups present within council practice, that is, groups formed for the discussion of issues of common concern over a sustained period of time, discussions in which participants' thoughts would be able to grow and develop through interaction and dialogue. Indeed, among the groups I studied, there were not even adult reading groups. This is in contrast to the fastest growing organization on the literacy scene, the Whole Language Umbrella, whose practice centers on the formation of this very kind of group.

Boxwood Council . . .

Mary passes out the data information sheets that members filled out at the last meeting, describing their interests and willingness to volunteer. As the group looks over the sheets, Mary reads a letter she received from a graduate student, at Francis College, who is offering to conduct workshops on Native Americans and "webbing," a reading technique.

"I spent last month doing Native Americans," says Valerie.

Mary adds, "She just finished her M.S. at Francis in English."

"What about a fee?" questions Karen.

"September is Native American month," Kathy nods.

"Wow, that would be great."

"How much do we have for programs?"

"About $100 for regular meetings. One meeting we do really cheap," answers Janet.

Kathy is pouring through her data sheets. "Everyone liked authors. There are three who want 'Make and Take' workshops."

The conversation continues to ebb and flow around the details of the possible upcoming events. They consider which groups of teachers each event will most appeal to, the days of the week members prefer to meet, and where they will hold the different events. In seeking to find a location for the dinner and speaker for the first evening, they name nineteen different area restaurants before the meeting is over. Soon calendars come out as they debate the merits of different dates, seeking to avoid holidays and other conflicts.

The conversation returns again to the author they will invite, as this is one of the more demanding and more expensive events they will present.

"Where could we get the money?"

"I think the Boxwood Community Foundation has $1,400 to give away."

"I don't know about this author. What has she written?"

"She and her husband have been researching African American history."

"Did she do the one about Harriet Tubman?"

"Wasn't that the black author we had in Springfield?"

At my suggestion, they discuss the possibility of publisher support and Valerie describes her experience working with bookstores and publishers. Kathy divides up some of the tasks for finding presenters and goes off to make a call, returning to announce that they've secured the graduate student who will make a presentation on Native Americans. Her only charge will be for handouts.

Cycles of Participation

There are many different ways that the council extends invitations to educators to join their group. While some members join based upon written material they have received—flyers or a newsletter—far more join because of a personal invitation. This invitation may come from a fellow teacher or principal who mentions the councils or buys a membership for a new teacher. It may come from a specialist or supervisor. College mentors frequently invite their students to join the organization.

For many, the impetus to join is to further one's knowledge about reading, but others joined initially to boost their council's membership numbers in order to assist the local group to maintain honor council status.

For educators who have had to change jobs frequently, the reading council can become an important stabilizing factor in their lives. The common values and the common forms of organization make the councils something that can be counted upon to be the same across diverse educational settings, and, through the councils, these members can continue to connect to former colleagues across the state.

Some members enter not through local pathways, but through state or national gateways. Local councils attract new members at each year's state conference. Thus, the quality of the state conference program is important to promoting local council membership. Some members also join IRA before they join the state and local councils. These tend to be people who are entering as college students rather than as teachers.

Once in, members participate in different ways, following different membership trajectories. Not all members progress to the deepest or most intense levels of participation: many are content to lurk at the edges of the circle. Members learn about the structure of the organization and how to perform the tasks required of different positions at different levels through forms of "legitimate peripheral participation" (Lave and Wenger 1991). They watch, they do, and they absorb; they serve as assistants, they listen to stories of what happened the last time the event was enacted, and they are directed. Indeed, much of the organization's traditions are oral, despite its literacy mission. The agenda, minutes, bylaws, and newsletter are its primary written documents.

The levels of participation in the councils are like the ripples that occur when you throw a rock in a pond. The farther away from the impact, the longer and slower the ripples, as they dissipate toward the banks. Closer to the impact the ripples are deeper, sharper, and more intense. So, too, with the councils—members furthest away from the impact are the most peripheral. As they draw closer to where "the rock fell," the circles of membership become more intense and focused. Each level of the reading council recruits from the levels of membership more peripheral to it.

Local Members: Outer Circle

Local members in the outermost circle may be no more than "paper members," simply paying their local dues and receiving a newsletter. Then again, they may attend one or all of the public events sponsored by the local group. Most of these members will be elementary or Chapter 1 teachers. They appreciate the fact that someone else is doing the planning for the events they attend but don't, can't, or haven't given thought yet to giving the time to be involved in the planning themselves. They may have only a very hazy idea of who is at the helm of their local council. They may know these leaders as names in the newsletter or faces who greet them at a local event. Local leaders may be teachers in their school or they may serve with them on committees in their district, and, in these ways too, they will gain greater knowledge of the leadership.

Because local membership includes state membership, these peripheral members will also receive the state newsletter and journal as part of their membership. Other than that, however, their connection to the state organization will be almost nil. They may attend the state conference, and, in fact, they may have been recruited at a state conference meeting. For peripheral members, state conference attendance will be mostly limited to the public sessions—workshops and lectures. They may sign up for a banquet or luncheon, but without friendly support, they may not even attend the public receptions. For these reasons, they may feel that the state organization's primary purpose is to produce the annual conference.

Local Members: Inner Circle

Locally involved members, like their more peripheral cousins, pay dues, receive newsletters, and attend public events. The locally involved member, however, has also begun to play a role in planning these events. Initially, one may serve as a committee member or assistant to an officer, or chair of one of the less demanding committees. These positions might include assistant to the membership chair, committee member for planning the reading fair, or chair of the Newspapers in Education Committee. In this role, entering members may attend the planning meetings of the local executive board. They will have more opportunities to meet the other local leaders, and they, in turn, will become known to other members. This is the first step to entering the inner circle of local leadership. Members at this level do not say, "I love it that others plan this," rather they speak of the "duty one has to give so that these events can happen."

Having progressed to this level, a member may plateau here for several years without cycling either further in or out of the organization. Once they have served in these roles, however, they will receive considerable pressure from the leadership to become an officer. In shifting to the next level of participation—holding an office—they will probably be assigned to the position of recording or corresponding secretary or treasurer. Members at this level may still have little sense of the state organization and its functioning other than the conference. Locally involved members do try to attend the state conference, attending many public sessions and some public receptions.

At the local level, positions are always filled by selection, never by contest. This was true of all the groups I observed. If you are asked to serve and agree, your name alone is put forward to the membership as the candidate for that position. Then, at one of the meetings, a vote is taken, and the results are inevitably unanimous. The reason given for the single candidate is generally that it is so difficult to find people to fill these positions.

Members always downplay their leadership role. "It must have been a weak moment when I decided to take this on," explained a member. It would be out of character to aspire to office. Stories about how one was selected or elected, at the local and state levels, emphasize the serendipitous nature of events—the role of chance and surprise—that led to their taking office. This indirect attitude toward taking up the reins of leadership is similar to what Arlene Kaplan Daniels found in her study of women civic leaders (1988).

In most councils today, becoming president is a three-to four-year commitment. The most formal, the four-year plan, is a mirror of the structure used at the state level. The first year, you serve as vice president elect, during which time you plan the programs for the year that you will serve as vice president or program chair. The second year, as vice-president, you supervise the events you planned. The third year you serve as president, presiding at the executive board meetings and attending the statewide board of directors' meetings in Bloomington, Illinois throughout the year. The fourth year you serve as past president, often with responsibilities for seeing that the group meets national honor council requirements. Local council presidents are often teachers, but this is also a position where one is apt to find teachers who are shifting to administration, administrators, or local college professors serving within the organization.

The position of president is a critical link between the local and state organizations. Through attending the statewide board of directors' meetings, local council presidents become aware of the structure and functions of the state group and come to know the state leadership as well as their cohort of local presidents. For many of the council presidents, their primary identification will be with their local group, and they will actually know few people at the state level unless these leaders have originally come from their area.

Local presidents represent their group at the state conference, attending and voting at the delegates' meeting. The largest, most active local councils may also send their local council president to the national IRA conference at the council's expense. This is usually tied to the fact that the council is receiving a national IRA Honor Council award, which the local council president will accept at the awards meeting. In these cases, the local council president will also begin to develop personal awareness of the IRA leadership. Because all local council officers must be IRA members, the president and other local officers will also receive the IRA newsletter throughout the year, as well as any selected journals for which they will pay extra to receive.

The greatest distinction between local members in the outer circle and those in the inner circle is the access that the inner circle members have to the executive planning meetings. At these meetings, members share their funds of knowledge (Moll et al. 1992) about schools and community services, literally knitting across these different areas of practice as they design council events. These funds of knowledge include such issues as what teachers want, where is a good place to hold an event, how one can get funding for an author, or what members of the outer circle have potential to move into the inner circle. The pooling of these funds of knowledge by members of this inner group represents an important form of social cognition that is distributed across the leadership group. In these planning meetings this social cognition is activated and the group serves as one large corporate entity.

Boxwood Council . . .

The conversation shifts to the state's Newspaper in Education project, which gets poor marks for sending the materials out so late in the year. The statewide leadership meeting in June, however, gets high marks for its practical applicability. Three of the members of this group will be retiring this year, taking advantage of the state's new early retirement policy, and there is an animated discussion of retirement options. Janet raises a problem she's been having cleaning the carpet in her basement.

Although all the local council board members are in place, they still have committee positions to fill, and on the data sheets they find the names of members who would like to become more involved in the running of the organization. They discuss different possibilities for including people.

Talking about the duties of the publicity chair leads to complaints about the publicity they receive from the local newspaper, and then the conversation circles back to the names of possible presenters. They consider librarians, as well as several names of well-known members from nearby local reading councils and members prominent in IRC.

"What about June Talbot?"

"You have to tell her—not the theoretical, the *practical*."

"What about a potpourri of whole language?"

"Did you know that the Stoneypoint District is totally whole language?"

"Who's the president of their council? Maybe they would present. Or, there's the state's whole language council."

The conversation moves back and forth from presenters to costs, from location to cost. Slowly they circle toward the making of decisions and the parceling out of responsibilities. As they close they elect to meet again in August. The chairs are pushed back. Valerie mentions how boring she finds the IRC Board of Directors' meetings. Karen asks if anyone is going to go to the Regional Reading Conference, jointly sponsored by IRC and IRA.

"I think they'll stop the regional conference. They've been arguing about whether it's valuable and who will pay. The attendance is really off," she comments.

We thank Janet, our hostess, and hurry out to the cars. Valerie and Karen wave to me as they drive away.

The Ties That Bind: Linking Local Councils to Other Layers of Activity

Connecting Local Councils with the State Organization

The president of each local council and each special interest council serves on the board of IRC. This means that five times a year they will join their colleagues, the other local council and special interest council presidents, zone coordinators, state committee chairs, and the executive board of IRC in Bloomington, Illinois, for the state board meeting. Altogether this makes for a board of over seventy people, a large group in which to conduct business.

The half-day meetings in Bloomington use the same agenda format as the local groups, but they are distinguished from local meetings by their higher level of formality, including the use of a trained parliamentarian. There is little side chatting during the meetings, unlike what occurs at local meetings. Discussions are timed by parliamentary procedure and votes are formal. Yet friends do have time to catch up with each other's news before and after the meeting and during the luncheon that follows the meeting.

Besides the regular meetings of the board of directors, there are a number of other structures that tie together local, state, and often national activities. Many of the committees that local councils appoint people to have statewide counterparts, such as the legislative committee and publicity committees. These committees are also a means of linking the local and state structures. Surprisingly, the one statewide committee mentioned most often at local council meetings was the Newspaper in Education Committee. The statewide leader of the committee, working in conjunction with newspaper people across the state, develops an annual newspaper-like publication on helpful hints for using newspapers in classrooms; it is distributed to all members in the organization. Discussion about the Newspaper in Education activities in local councils have to do with the pick up, distribution, and timing of this publication. I was never present at any substantive discussion of its contents. And, yet, at the meetings I attended, this procedural discussion took up more time and space than discussions about any of the other committees with local-to-state linkages.

Probably the strongest link between local and state council and local council and IRA is the structure of Honor Council, a national recognition program. Its requirements focus local councils toward participation in statewide activities, but even more so toward an emphasis on the increase of membership and promotion and publicity of the organization. As part of Honor Council, local councils are required to meet defined membership increase goals for local and IRA memberships and to promote membership at each council event. Optional promotional items include such events as contacting superintendents, local media, and local legislators, developing an image brochure, conducting a local advertising campaign for the group, and publicizing group activities. Presidents of local councils that meet these requirements are recognized at the annual state conference and the IRA conference. I attended the 1994 Honor Council assembly at the annual IRA conference in Toronto, a modest dessert affair. Members told me that in previous years council presidents were honored at a gala dinner banquet, but this was before the many mergers in the publication industry and the subsequent decrease in support for council extras.

Mention of Honor Council surfaces again and again throughout local council planning meetings. "And that meets an Honor Council requirement!" is a frequent refrain. Sometimes the relationship between activity and Honor Council requirement becomes inverted, with the Honor Council requirement serving as the impetus for the activity rather than as confirmation for an activity that grew out of council planning for local needs. Of all the means by which local councils connect to the state or IRA at the local planning level, the search to meet Honor Council requirements seemed to me to receive the greatest attention.

The Annual Statewide Conference

The purpose of the state organization, many would say, is to produce the annual conference. For many teachers in the state this may be their major professional development experience of the year. They enjoy the chance to hear nationally known speakers, meet educators from other parts of the state, browse in the exhibit hall, and attend the banquets and receptions. The conference, held in mid-April in the convention hall and surrounding luxury hotels in Springfield, Illinois, attracts a crowd of about three thousand from all parts of the state. It is a chance for teachers to get away from the classroom, be pampered, inspired, and gather new ideas for use with their students.

In a later chapter, I describe the experience of the state conference in careful detail.

IRA: A Distant Relative

Only a limited number of local and state council members are also members of IRA. As mentioned earlier, council bylaws require local officers to be IRA members, but this requirement has only recently begun to be strictly enforced. As part of IRA Honor Council requirements, each year local councils must meet a quota for IRA memberships, with a view toward increasing their participation in the national organization.

For the average local member, IRA is a very distant cousin to the organization they know and with which they work. In fact, in some cases IRA is a distant cousin of whom they may be unaware. It's not unusual for local members to lack an understanding of what IRA is or how it relates to IRC. They may even be fuzzy on what IRC is or how it relates to the local council with which they work. And, quite frankly, they often don't care. What they are interested in are practical ideas that will help them in their daily classroom work, not the ins and outs of organizational structure.

For those local members who are also IRA members, most will participate as "paper" members, receiving one or more publications and occasionally ordering an appealing title from the IRA publications catalog. These cascades of paper flow to all levels of the organization, not only informing members of events, but engaging them in a common cultural milieu. Many local members speak with pride of the publications they receive from the organization. For some it is an important professional badge of honor.

A small number of lucky members may have an opportunity, at some point in their career, to attend the IRA annual convention. The IRA convention closely resembles their own state conference in structure and content, but it is larger and glitzier with more national speakers, fancier receptions, and many, many more sessions and exhibits.

Only a handful of IRC members will participate in any deeper way with IRA staff, committees, or other activities. The state president, membership chair, and IRA representative will be most closely involved. Other IRC members serve on IRA committees or work with IRA special interest committees. Every year IRC members appear on the IRA conference program. If the IRA conference is held in Chicago, local program chairs will assist the national staff to conduct that affair, staffing different affairs and assisting with logistical arrangements.

As mentioned earlier, because of the size of the membership and the relatively high number of IRC members who are also IRA members (close to 50 percent), IRC represents a critical voting block in IRA elections. Those few IRC members who operate at the borderlands between IRC and IRA are well aware of this power. They aggressively market their selected candidate for IRA leadership, although they are not unique among state reading council organizations in so doing. IRC's national political strength has been a boon for IRA candidates from Illinois, and, consequently, in the past several years there have been a large number of Illinois members on the IRA Board of Directors, including Donna Ogle, Katherine Ransom, and Jerry Johns, all of whom received special support through *The Communicator* (the IRC newsletter). Since the completion of this study, Illinois member Katherine Ransom has also served as IRA president. The votes of local members who are also IRA members represent crucial electoral power.

Moving into IRC and IRA Leadership Circles
The inner and outer circles at the state and national/international level mirror, in many ways, the inner and outer circles of the local levels. You get your feet wet and show that you will follow through with responsibility by serving in various statewide committee capacities. Because the conference is such an important responsibility of the state organization, members who are seeking a more active role at the state level will soon gravitate toward planning of the statewide conference. This process is described in greater detail in a later chapter on the conference.

Conclusions

Knitting across practice is a skilled activity requiring many forms of knowledge and expertise. It is most successful when knitters have access to others, as the information and connections they need may be widely distributed among the community of reading teachers. The funds of knowledge they draw upon include information about the local, state, and national organization as well as local schools, curricular trends, local organizations, and sources of funding, publishers, and local businesses to name just a few.

Knitting across practice is more, however, than simply a means of networking for needed resources; it is also a means by which political goals and social issues work their way across various organizations and institutions. In the field notes presented in this chapter, the issue of multiculturalism presents an interesting case in regard to this phenomenon.

Throughout the meeting of the Boxwood Council, members discuss the need to engage speakers who will fulfill goals of what I have come to call the "social justice calendar" of the school year. They are eager to have a "black author" for Black History Month. They are pleased when they get an offer from a potential speaker who can offer a presentation on Native Americans. They mention the ways that they have been addressing the concerns of multiculturalism in their own classrooms. It is clear from the discussion that they believe the membership will also be vitally interested in this issue.

The multiculturalism or social justice curriculum portrayed here is an ancillary, enrichment curriculum to the school's core curriculum. This is not a drawback, however, as multiculturalism, as it is practiced here, is a school activity that maps nicely onto council goals and perspectives and, interestingly enough goes along with the new boom of interest in whole language approaches. With the various social justice weeks or months that are now standard addenda to the curricula has come a wave of new publications, including biographies, fiction attentive to racial, ethnic, and gender issues, and other forms of nonfiction. In schools, teaching this new curriculum means attending to the new children's literature and incorporating it into appropriate classroom activities. Publishers have been pleased to develop this new market niche and have been helpful in supporting reading councils and others to learn more about the materials and to purchase them. They do this through providing speakers or workshop leaders who will introduce the product to clients like reading council members.

Multiculturalism as it is practiced through the social justice calendar creates a punctuated ritual year, much like the ritual year of the reading councils. Council leaders know that providing a black author to speak to teachers during Black History Month is a simple solution to their scheduling dilemma and that the program will be well received by teachers. It is a much easier decision than trying to sort through the various language arts standards to develop a series of presentations about issues that may not be able to be packaged as "one good idea you can use tomorrow in the classroom."

As this example demonstrates, council practice, as it emerges at the interstices among various volunteers and their institutions and concerns, most easily incorporates those ideas that lend themselves to easy incorporation. Ideas that can be tagged as timely, packaged as a book to use in the classroom, or for which you can get outside financial support are appealing. As volunteer organizations, the reading councils are driven by a broad and encompassing mission, within which members are constantly in the process of shaping and adjusting activities to fit time constraints, members' interests, and changing educational concerns. Council practice is a never ending work in progress.

Note

1   Participation in the organization as a leader is closely tied to speaking events and speakers. Many leaders are speakers, that is, they give presentations at local council meetings and the state conference. As speakers, they develop a set of stock variations on topics such as successful practices they have developed in their classrooms, how to implement cutting-edge ideas (like whole language), new ideas from research, or they may be known for a kind of entertainment—humor, storytelling, or the like. The ebb and flow of speakers around the state is known among members as "the circuit."

    Experienced or old-time members play an important role as brokers of the circuit, that is, they help less knowledgeable members to find good speakers who meet the aims of their programs. This knowledge of speakers and the ability to broker these resources are highly valued. It may be one of the most important commodities that experienced members amass during their time in council work, and it is the knowledge that is highly valuable in building a leader's network among the various council groups.

Chapter 5

The Reading Sorority

During the 1994 IRA conference held in Toronto, I roomed with four other women, active members of local reading councils from another state. I knew them through my previous work in adolescent literacy issues. They had met each other through work at various times in their careers, and the annual IRA conference was the one time each year they could renew their acquaintanceship. This made the conference a "same time next year" experience for them. In addition to the circle of friendship, the conference and the hotel were a luxurious break from their responsibilities as senior teachers and leaders in their districts and the expectations of husbands and growing or grown children for their time and assistance. All four had attended numerous national conferences and were old hands at how to "do the conference."

On the first evening together, we sat around on the beds in our suite, poring over the program and pooling our resources—sharing what we knew about the program offerings, debating the merits of the various invitations they had received to publisher-sponsored events, and developing a schedule for the week that mixed sessions with numerous opportunities to socialize with the group. An important part of the schedule was "doing the exhibits."

Throughout the week my roommates were generous in showing me the ropes and sharing their stories of conferences past. As they did for each other, they included me in their invitations, saving me a chair at dinners and breakfasts and grabbing extra goodies for me at the exhibits. As we sat together at these events, we watched the unfolding procession, commenting on the other guests, pointing out reading celebrities, and gossiping about their backgrounds and the quality of their performance. In the evenings before bed, we talked about the day's sessions—whom we had seen and what had happened. My roommates told stories about their families or jobs and discussed mutual friends from past work and council experiences. I felt enveloped by a warm and supportive world, a world of women of similar age and background, a world of submerged and comfortable assumptions.

The very last evening, one of our group presented each of us with a tiny pin—a yellow pencil superimposed on a red apple. "This is for the reading sorority," she explained as she passed one out to each of us. The term struck me as particularly apt, not just for our group, but for the world of the reading councils. It captures the sense of an intimate, feminine world driven by a concern about reading, but a world in which reading has become one with mutually shared ideas about what it is to do and be an educator, woman, and citizen.

As I thought more deeply about the term *sorority* I realized that my actual knowledge of sororities was fragmentary and highly subjective. I myself had never been a sorority member and knew few people who had. Yet as I pooled my different sources of information, it seemed that my assumptions were probably not so dissimilar from those of the woman who had named our group "a reading sorority," a term that we all seemed to think fit so well.

In thinking about sororities and the characteristics I attribute to such organizations, I must first include something that could be labeled "the Greek ideal," a belief in the importance of education, service, and the group's role in furthering these ideals. The Greek ideal, as I define it, elevates the meaning of membership, assigning value and worth to what might otherwise simply be seen as an ordinary social group. Another characteristic of the sorority outlook would be a shared, deeply intuitive sense of who is and is not a member. This recognition is embodied in gestures, clothing, phrases, and other artifacts. It includes notions of gender, sexuality, race, and ethnicity. Finally, swirling around and through sorority life, I believe, is the richness of members' narrative lives, that is, the storytelling that members weave through the structures of organizations and events. Because the organization is primarily composed of women, those narratives are, for most intents and purposes, produced by and for women. These three characteristics will serve as the lens through which I view the reading sorority. Through the metaphor of the reading sorority, I seek to answer the questions, who are the members of this organization, and what is their relationship to it?

The Greek Ideal: A Passion for Education and Service

Participating as a member of the reading councils is participating in a community of people who agree to having a passion for reading and the teaching of reading.

You share a passion with other people for the teaching of reading . . . and when you keep going to these things, like at the Illinois Reading Council, you really feel a part of it. (Junior high school reading teacher)

It just reaffirms that no matter where you are there are some things about teaching and being with children or thinking about reading and thinking about children's literature that are very common. (Kindergarten teacher)

The thing I liked was that all the people had a common interest in the thing that they were involved and interested in—reading and reading instruction . . . It was kind of a melting pot—an eclectic group. They all have this common bond in reading but outside of that common bond they go everywhere, every which way. (Elementary school administrator)

The passion that council members refer to is composed of ideas about teaching, children, and literacy. The rationale for the passion implies a camaraderie that comes from shared knowledge of the world of schools. In members' discussion of this passion, the notion of reading comes across as a diffuse concept that can include many roles in relationship to reading. You can be a lover of reading, a teacher of reading, a reading specialist, an administrator concerned with the ways teachers support reading, a children's writer, or a textbook publisher. Each of these different positions or roles is related to each other by the shared passion for reading. Participating in the council attests to one's passion for these issues, and through participation one performs one's passion through the council's established rituals.

Members ground their shared passion for reading and the teaching of reading in their belief that reading is the foundation of all education. Not surprisingly, this notion also has been heartily touted by textbook publishers since the rise of the scientific study of reading, and it frequently threads its way through educational arguments in different policy arenas (Shannon 1989).

Reading's probably the most important thing that I'm teaching to the children. (Third-grade teacher)

To me there is absolutely nothing more important than reading. I think if you can read, you can at least self-teach yourself. (Second-grade teacher)

I think it [reading] is the key to all success in everything that they are going to do. (Third-grade teacher)

They all see the importance of reading and the impact that reading has on the total scope of education. And it really does—it's the thread that ties the whole thing together. (Administrator and longtime IRC member)

Teachers, often quite justifiably, believe that their profession is not held in high esteem in our society, as demonstrated by the many times they have heard, "Those who can do, and those who can't, teach." They feel that educators and education are unjustly expected to produce miracles of reform within complex social conditions. In this sense, the belief that reading is the foundation of all learning is a discourse of legitimization. As an aspect of the Greek ideal, this belief elevates mere teaching to new heights, giving reading instruction a deep cultural significance.

The belief in reading as the foundation of all learning is not only a reaction to criticism, it is also reflective of a vision. Members believe that reading, as a form of communication, is a major resource for making meaning of the world. Thus, through the teaching of reading, teachers "make" their students human, that is, they transmit to them the meaning-making skills that distinguish humans from other species. This view equates literacy with cognition and the uniquely human capacity for the creation of symbols.

> I consider reading and writing and literacy as thinking . . . and that's just the most valuable thing you can have in this world. We're all trying to make meaning out of life, out of everything we do, see, hear, think, and I feel that is what my big goal in school is. It sounds like it's right out of a book, but it is my innermost need, and teachers that I can feel a real connection with are those teachers that I can feel that their whole goal is that—to make sense out of the world and that's the most important thing I do with kids. Reading, writing, literacy—combining all of the curriculum into that goal is what I think is the most important thing. (Sixth-grade teacher)

For council members, reading is both a basic skill and the essential component of culture: it supports the well-rounded individual. "I feel for a human being to have a fulfilling life that literacy is a very vital part of that. That just watching television and listening to radio doesn't make a well-rounded person (Junior high school reading teacher)."

The belief in literacy as the basis for a well-rounded individual is loosely coupled to a belief in the "muchness" of literacy.

> I don't know that I've actually read what the official philosophy is, but I sort of think they [council members] feel that you can never ever read all there is. You can never know all there is, but just sitting back and not doing anything about it doesn't help you at all. By going out and reading and finding out more—that definitely helps you and makes you grow, no matter in what area, whether it's religion or math or language or just reading for enjoyment. Whatever you read you learn something from it. And it makes you grow and be a better person or a more knowledgeable person at least. And if you have children, the more you read, the more you can help them. (Second–third-grade teacher)

For the well-rounded individual, the ability to read is not enough. There always is the need to exercise that skill. Reading in this sense is an active, dynamic process which is always in a state of formation, and because of this ongoing process of formation, it can never be viewed as complete—one is always searching for more. This view of reading has, to my mind, strong parallels to religious views of Christ, views in which his sacrifice and goodness can never be truly appreciated by mortals. Christian faith must then always be an unfulfilled affair, one that relies upon trust in the Lord, powered by a constant search for knowledge that one will never fully possess. In like fashion, council members regard the value, truth, and importance of literacy as something that we must always have faith in and exercise to our greatest potential, but it is a phenomenon which we will never fully understand nor attain. (The relationship between members' views of literacy and religion I discuss in more detail in chapter 7.)

For the reasons stated above, council members see reading as a double-hinged proposition. Personal success and happiness accompanies successful learners, while personal unhappiness and social and economic liabilities are the fate of unsuccessful learners. Council members find evidence for these beliefs in their own experiences with children who fail as readers. These sad stories create an urgency to their sense of mission about reading.

> I went with reading because I had volunteered for the GED program and for the adult literacy program. I used to do that one night a week, and there was such a need. There were so many adults in this adult literacy program that were not second language learners. . . that is, they had been, you know, in the United States, and had not learned to read. They were brilliant! I mean bright, bright people. And for years they had figured out lots of ways to do everything, but didn't read. So I just thought that was criminal. We just cannot do that. We've got to get to our children, and we've got to get them when the time is ready, because these people were struggling terribly, but the desire was there. (Third-grade teacher)

Members' personal beliefs about reading and the importance of councils' work are integral to their views of the organization and its purpose. Members speak of the organization as a "collection of interests," one which does not advocate any one position or philosophy. They believe that this outlook distinguishes them from advocacy organizations that take a particular position or philosophy at the expense of others. Being a collection of interests, rather than an advocacy organization, is a strength, they believe. It makes them "broader" than an organization like the Whole Language Umbrella, which "only deals with whole language." In discussing the issue of their philosophy or purpose, members frequently used the term "smorgasbord" to describe what the organization offers members. "It allows for differences of opinion, but the same goal," stated one teacher. Indeed, questions about organizational philosophy prompt a range of denials, from "We don't talk about that kind of thing" and "We don't have one philosophy that I know of" to a simple "I don't know." Or as one IRA staff member said to me, "We're so diversified. We offer something for everyone. We don't have to defend anything, stand for any one thing" (IRA staff member, personal communication, June 1993).

Despite their denial of a common philosophical base, members do seem to be moved by a collective impulse, the parts of which they can readily identify. One part of this collective impulse, discussed earlier, is their shared emphasis on reading and its importance. They also believe that they are headed in a similar direction in their beliefs about what makes for good reading instruction. They state this in a number of ways. "We're all moving toward whole language" is the most common statement, but they also refer to this direction as "literature-based classrooms," "literature in the classrooms," "inquiry-driven classrooms," and "holistic philosophy." "I think they are basically moving toward the whole language philosophy. Most seem to want to stress reading for enjoyment, getting children to enjoy the literature. Teaching for meaning versus, as was done before with the phonics, teaching the little parts first and not getting to the whole" (Chapter 1 teacher and local council official).

Members also share a common sense of how one reaches these goals. This common sense is in close keeping with their belief in the organization's purpose as a collection of diverse interests, not as an advocacy group that stands behind a monolithic outlook: "It's kind of what works for you, and there's good in all ways. You kind of pick and choose. Just like with whole language, you know? You sort of go one way and then you go another. That's kind of the trends of the last ten years. I don't think anyone's going to say, 'This is the right way.' You just see what the results are as you go down the road" (Third-grade teacher).

"Picking and choosing," "finding one good idea," "using what works for you"—these are all phrases that are emblematic of the ways members believe they should make use of what they learn from council events. They are embedded in the belief of the council as a collection of interests.

Surprisingly, the passion that members say they feel about reading is coupled with a sense of world weariness about the particulars of reading pedagogy. When posed with questions about reading and the councils, members often reply, "There's nothing new in reading," or "What goes around comes around." This stance of "I've seen it all before" is a special marker of group membership. First, it signals their participation in a field that toughens people up quickly by the hard experience of the ups and downs of classroom and school life. Second, it proclaims their longevity in that field. Third, this stance indicates their solidarity with their fellow educators. Their comradeship stems, in part, from the knowledge they share of schools and education and the changes that have occurred in schools over the last couple of decades.

"What goes around comes around," however, also serves as a way to preclude discussion about the new—filtering out the meat of new issues by defining them as "something that we've really encountered before." When used in this way, new ideas, for instance from whole language, are quickly catalogued as analogous to old ideas, like language experience. When leaders within the organization make such proclamations about the new, they direct members toward business as usual and away from reflective processes that might threaten the accepted structure.

This seemingly innocuous phrase, "what goes around comes around," is highly emblematic of what it is to be a member. It says that we are grassroots teachers; we work in the trenches day in and day out. We know children and are at the heart of making things work in schools. The phrase speaks to the great amount of experience that these teachers have amassed. It also, however, demonstrates the conserving forces that are at work shaping teachers' definitions of themselves and their work.

Members' literacy beliefs can be stated in something like the following creed: What is special about our group is that we share a passion for the teaching of reading, which is the foundation for all learning. Indeed, reading is the most important thing you can teach a child in school. This means that teachers who teach reading are doing essential work and, for that reason, are deserving of our nation's regard and respect. Children who learn to read will be more likely to grow up to be good citizens, find decent jobs, and live happy and productive lives. There's always room to grow as a reader, and there is always more to read. We've chosen this as our mission because we've seen it all—children falling through the cracks, and adults who never had a chance. There are many paths that one can follow to meet these goals, and we do not presume to know which one is right for you. We lay out the possibilities for our members, and they choose which will work best for them. We don't support any one philosophy—we are a collection of broad interests. And, don't think you can fool us or surprise us by barraging us with new, foolproof reading methods, because what goes around comes around, and we've probably seen it before in one form or another.

Insiders and Outsiders: The Traits of Membership

Earlier, in discussing the cycles of participation within the organization, I referred to members who were insiders and outsiders in regard to the structure of the organization. There also is a distinction between insiders and outsiders in regard to the traits of membership.

Judy: How would you characterize the members?
Gordon: They're all female.
Judy: [I laugh] That's true isn't it.
Gordon: I'm the only male in every group. There may be one male or two male principals that may come a few times during the year, but otherwise . . . They're female. I'd say they are either first year teachers or middle-aged. They are mostly middle-aged women. Um . . . These are all physical kinds of things . . .
Judy: Yeh, but these are . . .
Gordon: . . . the things you notice right off the bat . . .
Judy: Right. Anyone could walk in and see this immediately.
Gordon: As I said earlier, it seems like they are active in the community and active in their buildings. When you talk to these different members over the years, one of the common threads that I've found is that they are involved with some kind of project or program at the school, that they are the person that's either leading or involved in some type of enrichment group, or some type of new reading program, that they are the person that seems to know more about what's going on in a certain program than other teachers. So, they're the person, I guess, you go to when you want answers because they've been trying stuff. They've been experimenting. I don't know. I think the age, the middle age and the women are what I notice the most. And I guess maybe that's why I stand out.
Judy: Do you think, has that ever given you the sense that it directs the council activities into certain kinds of formats or into certain directions?
Gordon: Definitely. I guess the other big thing, beside the couple I just mentioned, is that they are mostly primary teachers—primary up to 4th grade. You never see a high school teacher or a middle school teacher at any of the meetings. So, I think, when you're planning your meetings, you gotta know your audience. And it's lower grades. So you've got to find something that

thrills the "make and take" crowd, and that's the lower elementary. (Former elementary teacher, administrator, and longtime council member)

As a male, Gordon is an outsider in the reading sorority, and, yet, paradoxically, as an elementary teacher, he is also an insider. Both his insider and his outsider status inform him about important membership characteristics. Understanding what is inside and what is outside, in terms of membership traits, is critical to participating effectively and happily within the fold of the reading councils. While members can talk about many of the attributes, there are many others of which they are unconscious. Gordon mentions some of the most obvious here—the age, gender, and teaching status of members, that is, that they are middle-aged women working in the primary grades. He is also aware that reading council members are apt to be more active members of the teaching corps, with deeper professional interests than many of their school colleagues. As another member put it to me, "These are the teachers that you miss when they are out of the building."

It is not only that outsiders identify these qualities of council members, it is an important part of members' identities as members that they view these characteristics as part of their makeup. Being "active" is an important part of that identity. In line with that attribute, members also speak of each other as "positive" rather than "negative" kinds of people. They explain that good members are "hard workers" and "always willing to lend a hand." Members label the attributes of active, positive, and hardworking as "forward looking," which they view as the opposite of "reflective," a term that is sometimes mentally coupled with inactivity, backward looking, or even negativity.

Judy: What have you liked about being involved in the local council? You've done it three years now . . . What has been satisfying about it?

Sandra: The group of people on the board of directors. That is one of the hardest working, intelligent, industrious group of people that you could ever work with. It's the kind of thing that as president, and I observed this as vice president, everybody had a job to do and everybody did it. As president I did not have to go to somebody and find out why something wasn't done.

Judy: It was done.

Sandra: They did their job, and you would come to a meeting and you would have a concern or a problem or something that appeared from the state meeting that as president I had attended, and you'd go back to the council and say, "Well, this has come up." Or, "We're going to have . . . we have a problem with this. This has happened." And immediately you would have a brainstorming of ideas and all sorts of alternative solutions to that by these people who are chairs of their respective committees. And that's what I enjoyed about it. Good natured! I mean, you've been there.

Judy: It's great fun.

Sandra: Yes, it really is. It's a lot of work, but it was made pleasurable by the group of people who were willing to serve on that board of directors. (Local council official)

Sandra's comments find echo in many of the formal and informal interviews I had with members. Valued members work hard, shoulder their load, and complete their responsibilities as expected. Moreover, working hard and working together makes the work fun. Sandra and her cohort, buoyed up by their sense of mutual productivity, look forward to being together.

Alluded to in Sandra's interview is the very important attribute of "getting along with others." Within council life, there is a very strong prohibition against open or direct conflict. "There is an ethic of working together in IRA. There is very little pull and tug" (IRA staff member). "They are not an argumentative group" (Local council member).

This is not to say that conflict does not occur, especially at the higher levels where the political stakes are much greater, but those who engage in open conflict are often censured by the general membership. Ironically, my file of field note fragments on council conflicts is one of the thickest I possess, and yet, from members' perspectives, conflict is not a desired quality.

Being a Teacher: Being a Woman

The issue of council membership and identity never strays far from the issue of the identification of oneself as a teacher. "All of them are still teachers, even if they're not still a teacher, I think. Whatever they do, they're teaching something to somebody, even if they're not a teacher. Does that make sense to you? They still have that teacher mentality of . . . I have to . . . I care about kids. I care about reading. I think that's pretty universal" (Longtime council member and school administrator).

As the comments of this council member demonstrate, being a teacher is not only a professional title, it is also a body of knowledge about ways of being, gestures, and habits that follow one into other areas of life. In other words, being a teacher is embodied.

Because to be an elementary teacher is, for most intents and purposes, to be a woman, the embodiment of this teacher identity is deeply intertwined with gender issues. Female council members identify themselves simultaneously as teachers and as women, the lines between the two blending easily, one constituting the other. An example of this blended identity is demonstrated in the ways female teachers physically inscribe themselves as educators, particularly as reading educators.

One afternoon as I was walking down the hallway of an elementary school on my way to a council meeting, I suddenly realized that the symbols of school, which I saw all around me on the walls, were the same symbols that I had seen so many teachers wearing as various pieces of clothing and accessories—pins, earrings, T-shirts, sweatshirts, vests, and other items. These symbols were of two sorts: (a) idealized symbols of school such as red apples, open books, little red schoolhouses, and yellow pencils; (b) the thematic symbols of the holidays and seasons that schools celebrate, from Halloween and fall to Christmas, Valentine's Day, and snowy days; and (c) the emerging symbolism of multiculturalism or the social justice curriculum—clasped white and black hands, a flock of varegated children, or a rainbow with a slogan. Teacher clothing and jewelry containing these symbols are hot items at any reading council presentation or conference exhibit.

Besides the ritual symbols, many of the pieces of teacher clothing also sport snappy messages related to teaching. These might include such phrases as "Teachers are A+" or "Pop Quiz today!" I myself have a large collection of T-shirts with reading messages that range from "Only Reading Makes It Real" and "The More You Read the More You Grow" to "Win with Reading" and "Building a Community of Readers." I also possess handbags, buttons, mugs, lamps, playing cards, and a flashlight with messages about reading. My very favorite pieces of teacher clothing, however, are the many nightshirts that I have seen for sale at reading conferences with messages about "teachers as lovers." Here is one of the longest and most involved texts I've discovered:

Teachers Make Great Lovers
They believe in a hands-on approach featuring a variety of manipulative play activities that utilize both fine and gross motor skills. They will excite you with tactile stimulation and body imaging. It will be a highly creative experience, incorporating imagination, visual perceptions, and sensory-motor integration. All

of these activities are developmentally appropriate, and, if you don't get it right the first time, they make you do it again and again . . . until you do! FINALLY . . . if you are REAL good you get milk and cookies afterward!

Although this T-shirt message does not refer explicitly to women as the teachers who are lovers, female gender is implied in many subtle ways. Moreover, the majority of teachers are female, and these T-shirts are sold to teachers, at conferences at which women predominate. The mention of "milk and cookies" makes a strong connection to the teachers of young children, again primarily women.

The multiple messages about schooling and women mentioned above circulate through the lives of council members. They encounter them on the walls of the school, they use the same symbols to decorate the newsletters produced by the reading councils, and they wear them on their bodies. The symbols intertwine visions of the mythic time of the golden age of schools, the passing of the seasons as charted by the calendric cycle of the school year, the slogans of a positive and competitive culture of reading, and the emergence of a national movement for multiculturalism. Together they create a powerful iconographic universe in which literacy, gender, and professional roles are powerfully portrayed.

Male and female members are highly aware of the stylistic differences between the genders. Male council members, as I learned, recognize that men and women participate in different ways, but men are often reluctant to discuss these differences. When they do, they may refer to these differences, as this principal, George, did, as differences in habits and approaches, not as discrepancies between power and role:

George: The other thing that is really depressing is that there is not really very many men involved in this thing, and I don't think that it's from a lack of them trying.

Judy: Um . . . what do you think kind of keeps them out of being involved?

George: Well, one, the number of male teachers is probably less than the number of female teachers.

Judy: Yeh.

George: I find that it's kind of different that there are so few administrators involved in the thing.

Judy: Um . . . there have been other principals or administrators in the past, but it sounds like there are few now.

George: As far as I know. And that seems different to me.

Judy: Um-hm. So you get the sense that it is both a very Teacher-dominated and, as part of that, a very Female-dominated organization.

George: And I don't think that's necessarily bad. It's just the way it is. It isn't bad . . . the male-female thing.

Judy: But how are female organizations different from male organizations? Not having been on the other side—and you have been on both sides. If this were a group of male teachers, would they do it differently?

George: You want me to be sexist?

Judy: I don't see it as sexist. I'm just really curious to see—how might they have done business differently?

George: I'm trying not to be sexist, alright?

Judy: OK. And this is also anonymous.

George: OK.

Judy: So, don't feel . . .

George: OK, well, I think women worry about the little things a lot. When I meet with the principals of other schools, who happen to be male . . . we don't necessarily talk about the little things, they just get taken care of.

Judy: When you say little things, can you give me an example?

George: Like what kind of food we're going to have.

Judy: [I laugh.] Now, of course, that's a major concern.

George: Don't discuss it, just do it! What time and where exactly we're going to put the tables, and all those things. And I suppose those are important, but they don't move the meeting along very well . . . It's not something you need to have everybody talk about.

Judy: Um-hm. Well, if that wasn't the focus of the meeting, what kinds of things would be the focus of the meeting?

George: I just want to know what's going on, who is doing it, if you have questions, what each person did—what a report is supposed to be about, "Yeh, I did this, and this is what I'm planning to do." And then go on.

Judy: So, you don't think that if this were a group of men that they would be talking about different issues . . . they would still be talking about the same issues, but they would do it in a different way.

George: Yeh, I think so.

Judy: It's not that they would talk about completely different issues,
         or be planning completely different kinds of activities?
George: No, I don't think so. I think the activities that they've done are
         fantastic. I think they just . . . I don't know . . . that sounds
         really bad.

In an organization composed primarily of women, time and attention
is spent on the procedural details of work that, in organizational and
family life, tends to fall to women. After all, these details are the position
from which these women view life. However, while George finds the discussion of such detail irksome, he essentially agrees with the focus and
content of council planning meetings, that is, he does not envision a
different kind of organization with different kinds of goals and discussions.

It is not only the manner of participation, but also the traditions of
council life that are gendered. References to tradition are, in many re-
spects, veiled references to distinctions of gender and power, as many
female council members are well aware. Some female members complain
about the male members of the council, often school administrators, who
are resistant to what they perceive as changes to council traditions. Part
of that tradition, these women say, is the male right to treat female council members as "one of their teachers."

These same women also realize that many of their female colleagues
are, whether consciously or unconsciously, compliant with these roles.
"You take a look at the districts across this state . . . and the overwhelm-
ing majority of those local reading councils are all women and those
women, for the most part, are still disposed to relate to the papa figure in
their building," explained a longtime female member. Tradition relates to
gender and relates to power in complex fashion. All three elements are
constitutive of the practice and the subjective identities of the participants to that practice.

Difference and the Null Theory of Membership

Just as one is identified by what one is or what membership characteristics one possesses, one can also be identified by what one isn't or what
one fails to possess. As I grew into council practice, I learned much about
the characteristics of good members—people were eager to tell me. However, it was often by innuendo, silence, or absence that I learned about the
null theories of membership. These are the criteria for what members are
not.

Over time, I learned that as important to membership as your behavior was your racial, religious, and sexual orientation. For instance, as I attended meeting after meeting I saw few, if any, nonwhite members. When I asked about this, the responses I got were often delivered in hushed tones, making me feel that by raising the issue I had done something indelicate, crossing a silent line of inappropriateness.

Other forms of knowledge about difference and membership appeared in small epiphanic moments. For instance, I attended a potluck for a council leadership group at which the hostess served a pork dish as the main entree. It is not unusual to serve pork in the Midwest, but I wondered about the assumption that everyone present would be able to eat pork.

At another meeting, a facilitator turned to me as the group was beginning to form and said as an aside, "I could ask them to start with a prayer, but it would be just my luck there would be someone Jewish in the group." She explained that she had just come away from several weeks of teaching at a summer Bible study camp. Having been deeply schooled in the notion of separation of church and state, I was surprised that she would consider prayer an appropriate activity for what was an ostensibly nonreligious educational group. Again, my sensibilities were jarred. This incident, along with other incidents, helped to alert me that a certain Christian perspective was an unstated norm of the group.

Eating lunch with a mixed group of council members, men and women, a man repeated a joke that his school administrator had told him. "We used to say 'birth to death' or 'womb to tomb,' but now with AIDS we say 'erection to resurrection.'" Why does he assume that these kinds of sexuality issues can be discussed in mixed company, I asked myself. Is he also making an assumption about the group members' sexual orientations, that is, that we can make these comments because no one in this group will have AIDS and no one in the group is gay? My puzzlement caused my sensitivity indicator to jump another notch.

These incidents and others told me about the things no one really wanted to discuss, which are that council members are generally white, Protestant, and not gay. It is such a given that you can bank on it as safe to live and speak as if those outside these categories were actually not present, whether or not you know this is so. In this sense, these titles—white, Protestant, straight—are labels that categorize *and* practices that are lived.

It would not be fair to go further without mentioning that on a policy level IRA has been, from its beginnings, a strong and outspoken supporter of civil rights issues. From its inception the organization has had a policy not to book hotels or hold its conferences in cities where racial discrimination is openly practiced. In addition, IRA barred national affiliates with membership clauses that would discriminate against potential council members on the basis of race. As demonstrated by the previous chapter, members are aware of and seek to be responsible to national calls for attention to diversity. On a less conscious level, however, there are embodied contradictions.

Many reading council members deem criticism of their organization and practice on the grounds that they are homogeneous or exclusive as unfair. They protest that the reading councils are highly diverse. They seem baffled that others cannot see or appreciate this diversity. Many spoke to me of the difficulty of meeting all of the needs of such a diverse group. To their minds diversity is present because people from different geographic areas participate, but even more so because there are teachers who teach at all grade levels, as well as people in administrative or university positions. Grade-level differences and organizational position are, for them, important markers of diversity. They also consider their organization's willingness to provide a forum for a broad spectrum of reading beliefs or methods as further proof of diversity. In this sense, they choose to define diversity as a selected range of member attributes without reference to specific attributes of race or ethnicity.

Another way that council members and their leaders translate the meaning of diversity is as a kind of internationalism, something like a parade of national flags. In this sense, they believe they are actively striving to ameliorate racial and ethnic barriers through active internationalism. Local councils are urged by their state and national leaders to buy memberships for teachers from other countries' teachers who may be too poor to buy their own. One of IRA's five goals is to further international development: "Identifying, focusing, and providing leadership on global literacy issues." Most IRA members live in the United States or Canada, but news from international affiliates receives high priority in *Reading Today,* the organization's national newspaper. The newspaper also highlights information about projects in which local councils work with or support international affiliates through book drives or similar community projects. Supporting international participation serves as a surrogate multiculturalism policy that promotes surface awareness of differences but fails to address deeper levels of practice that may actively discourage the presence of those who do not represent the membership status quo.

Although many council members may not be aware of it, and those who are may not be eager to speak of it, there are pockets of resistance within the councils, where questions about difference and the organization's focus have been raised. These are the voices of women, reported above, who are acutely aware of the power issues being played out through gender. In Illinois, a group of members recently led an active protest against the scheduling of the joint IRC-IRA Midwestern regional reading conference on one of the important Jewish holidays. This protest led to the formation of the statewide organization's ad hoc committee on multicultural affairs.

Caring and Sharing: Narrative Worlds

Council meetings, particularly the more intimate and smaller executive planning meetings, but, indeed, all events, provide important opportunities for members to weave the stories of their own lives into the proceedings. Members place high value on this aspect of council life. Indeed, members of the state executive committee identified a period of IRC leadership as particularly rocky by reference to the way that committee meetings had been too businesslike and devoid of the personal caring they value so much. They were pleased that they seemed to be getting back to a more personal style of meeting, in which "everyone cares about everyone else." An important aspect of this caring is the willingness to provide space in the meetings for personal anecdotes and to engage with others outside of meetings for the sharing of stories. To listen to the personal tellings is a sign of solidarity.

Personal tellings come in many forms, depending upon the forum, the audience, and the topic. Within meetings, a personal telling may be a one-line reminder, a joke, or a quick anecdote. At a local council planning meeting I heard this exchange:

> "I want you to know that there is no such thing as an LD [learning disabled] student," Barbara tells the executive committee of the Prairie Council, with an air of ironic authority. The group is finishing dinner, seated at a table in a far corner of a national restaurant chain.
>
> "Where did you hear that?" someone challenges her, scoffingly.
>
> "On 'Penny for Your Thoughts'." [This is a radio program.]
>
> "There's no such thing as an LD student," repeats Barbara. "It's just teachers who don't know how to teach."
>
> This prompts a number of angry comments from the group about the criticism teachers receive from an often ill-informed media. (Field notes from local council planning meeting)

There are also times and places for longer stories. At one community service event I attended, members worked shoulder to shoulder sorting books to distribute as Christmas presents to needy children. Here stories of a more personal nature were spun out at greater length, describing the networks of caring that members maintained for a disabled husband, an errant son, and an elderly mother.

Ironically, as members of one council worked to reproduce the ritual of Christmas giving for children in their community who might not normally receive books as presents, they spoke with a mixture of chagrin and pride about the roles they play as women in reproducing this ritual in their own families. "Why does Christmas always have to be a woman's holiday," said someone with irritation, and the group muttered agreement. They spoke of the responsibility, the preparations, and the exhaustion they felt over the holidays. Responsible for the purchase of almost all the gifts for wide circles of friends, family, and work acquaintances, they traded sweet and sour stories of the mistakes they had made in selecting presents for different relatives. The stories combined an element of irritation blended with aspects of pride in the role they occupy as the nurturers of so many.

While many of the stories that members tell are about their personal lives, many more are about their lives in schools and their lives as teachers. These reflect the atmosphere of teaching in schools today. I was surprised to note the number of stories I had gathered that dealt with teachers' lack of autonomy and job insecurity. Members described the cavalier way their teaching assignments were made and then changed at the last minute, often with no input from the teacher. Generally, these reassignments reflected administrator's needs, not the skills, experience, and desires of the teacher in question. A decade of building a personal classroom library of hundreds of volumes and a wealth of materials for teaching specific curriculum topics all geared to the third and fourth grade would become an irrelevant asset one afternoon when a teacher was suddenly assigned to a kindergarten classroom.

In one council's area, the closure of a major industry caused large demographic shifts and changes in the tax base. Members who had taught for many years in that district suddenly risked losing jobs that they had assumed were assured until retirement. During that time, they spoke of the fear and dread they felt and the physical symptoms of stress they experienced as they waited to know if they would be rehired. Members with secure positions listened and comforted their friends, urging them not to worry. The sense of fear engendered by the district changes demonstrated the critical role these teachers played as breadwinners in their families. Their salaries were essential in paying home mortgages, children's college tuitions, and parents' homebound care.

Members also spoke of mandates from state or national sources, mandates that affected their lives. Because so many reading council members are Chapter 1 teachers, their teaching lives are closely connected to the ins and outs of those federal regulations. In addition, federal, state, and district concerns interconnect in a number of ways. For instance, in Illinois, Reading Recovery, an early intervention program developed in New Zealand and exported to the United States, was receiving wide publicity and promotion as a model for Chapter 1 programming. Many districts had converted their entire Chapter 1 program into the Reading Recovery model, insisting that all Chapter 1 teachers undertake the rigorous one-year training program and adhere to this approach. While teachers noted many good things about this program, they also shared many stories about their concerns with it. The training, they believed, sought to convert them as disciples rather than to respect and build upon the years of teaching experience they brought to the program. Some teachers refused to take the training because of this issue, switching to classroom positions: others, in anger, dropped out of the training midway. Members worried about the numbers of children in the older elementary grades for which there were now no services, as Reading Recovery is geared primarily to first graders. "Some kids just aren't ready then," a twenty-five-year Chapter 1 veteran explained. "They just need more time." Members also spoke of the cost to districts of working one-on-one when they were sure, from their own experience, that they could create an equally effective program working with small groups. Where, I wondered, in all of the statistical claims of effectiveness for this program are the voices of these experienced practitioners represented?

Council meetings, the small executive committee meetings, the events where members chatted before and after, or the conferences—these were all important occasions for sharing programmatic information and critiques. In these ways, members were alerted to the problems they might face when an issue hit their district. They had case-study knowledge of the issue and information on resources for dealing with it.

Much of what members talked about in describing the atmosphere of schools had to do with their intimate work with children. While there were some stories of children's learning, there were many more of the problems that children in dire circumstances face, and the role that teachers must take in these matters. Glinda, an experienced elementary teacher, spoke one evening with great tiredness of a seriously disturbed child in her class, one whose acts took all of her energy and attention to monitor. "It's the worst year I've ever had," she said, her shoulders sagging in defeat. Because of jurisdictional disputes, she explained, they were unable to get the child special services. At another meeting, two teachers from the same school described how their elementary school had been vandalized by a pair of young teenagers who had been long-term school failures. The teens had broken into the cafeteria, smeared catsup and mustard on the walls, and then broken into the library, smashing a computer into smithereens. There was sadness around the table when members shared stories about the knowledge young children brought to class about adult sexual relationships or violence. And that violence seeped into their own lives. As one urban council member described: "We've had the police up there. We've got weapons problems. We have gang problems . . . You know, there's a lot of violence. And it's difficult for people to deal with. It's difficult for myself to deal with . . . You know, I feel for the kids I work with because the communities they are coming from are failing them in my mind . . . We feel, gee, if we can just get them through the day getting them lunch without being hurt, that's almost a successful day, and that's not exactly why I went into this business."

However, all was not so bleak. Overall, as I looked back at the many snippets of personal talk that were threaded through my observations, I was struck by the role that humor or fun played in council members' storytelling. Humor is lodged in the bowels of teacher knowledge. They love to laugh about the funny incidents of classroom and school life—a child's comment about reading, a teacher's foible, or a quip about administrators. These stories came from their deep and shared knowledge of the institution, the roles, and the patterns that characterize their professional lives.

They also appreciate ironic humor, a product of the practicality they have to demonstrate in their roles as teachers. One teacher described a very difficult boy who very skillfully played his two divorced parents and his social worker off against her, his teacher. He was depending upon the difficulty that the concerned parties had in contacting each other to make quick and agreed-upon reactions to his behavior. In response, this teacher brought her portable phone to school. At the next infraction, she pulled it out of her purse and, to the young man's horror, immediately called one of his parents, who quickly reprimanded him. Members responded to the telling of this story with deep chuckles of admiration for this teacher.

Although fun occurs sometimes within caring, members seldom told stories of doing things for the sake of fun. Fun and humor are embedded in duty. When they participate in holidays, it is as the organizers of the ritual events—preparers of the food, buyers of the gifts, inviters of the guests. When they attend sports events, it is as companions to their husbands or as supporters of the schools at which they teach or the communities in which they reside. They sit by the side of men to cheer teams of boys or men. When they participate in athletics, which is seldom, it is to lose weight, reduce stress, or keep a younger looking figure; it is not to gain skill and experience physical excitement. For council members, duty reigns.

Even though they are emblematic of duty, council activities also provide a number of ways to escape duty. The annual conference is one such example. Here members are momentarily freed from the daily expectations of classroom or home. Here they can dance and sing at a karaoke party, play carnival games at a publisher-sponsored reception, or spend an evening in a hotel room with other council members, laughing about the pretensions of the "heart throbs" of the reading world. But here, too, the release is an attribute of the duty, as if to say, "After all, we are here because of reading; release is a celebration of our duty."

Conclusions

The reading sorority wraps its members in warm, encompassing folds of activity, fellowship, and commitment. These folds include the shared ideals about education and service, the deeply embodied knowledge of membership traits, and the narratives of sharing and caring that are so important to why members like to participate. Some of the knowledge about structure, membership, and participation can be read about, some is told, but much of it must be lived to be learned.

Being a good council member means far more than simply believing in the importance of learning to read. It also extends deeply into the kind of person you are, your clothing, bearing, and style of interactions, not to mention your gender, race, and sexual orientation. In the next chapters, I will explore the ways that knowledge about membership intertwines with ways of thinking about reading and practicing as a reading professional.

Chapter 6

The Expert Presentation

The place of teachers' professional associations remains nearly invisible in the main stream professional development literature. We know little about the role played by the largest and most prominent subject matter associations (NCTE, NCTM, NSTA, and others) in the professional lives of teachers or in shaping teachers' disposition toward particular reforms—J. Little

The most prevalent form of professional development offered by local councils is the expert presentation: It is the dominant genre. When council members elect to attend such events they have two requirements: (a) that they "will feel better than when they arrive" and (b) that they will have "just one new idea to use the next day in the classroom." If these two goals are met, then the expert presenter will be considered a success. An administrator clarifies these expectations: "You really get a chance, in your own backyard, to hear great speakers, and you didn't have to drive sixty miles to a conference. You can hear someone and you've taken two hours or an hour and a half out of your evening, and you can go back the next day and try all this stuff. It's not drained you, and you didn't spend a lot of money. It's a very low cost way to really get pumped up and to go back and try a bunch of stuff."

As mentioned in an earlier chapter, expert presenters can be teachers or administrators. College professors frequently serve in this role. Children's authors and other presenters such as professional storytellers are also highly desired expert presenters. Expert presenters are often members with at least state-level involvement in the reading councils, and many are "on the circuit" to audiences outside of their state.

Expert presenters have to "have a schtick" as one member described it to me. They may be a classroom teacher who can provide hands-on details for how to implement a new reading reform, or they may be a college professor who argues for a new reading technique, such as Sustained

Silent Reading. Children's authors describe how they came to write the books they wrote or why reading is so important for children or themselves. If one wishes to remain on the circuit this schtick will change over the years adapting to new issues and interests in the reading world. Many sought-after speakers have a couple of speeches that they can give on different reading topics, adapting their presentation to the audience's needs.

While the topics presented may change, what does not change, however, is the genre of the expert presentation, that is, the loosely defined rules and expectations that structure this form of presentation.

In this chapter, I explore an exemplar of the expert presentation genre. My aim is to dissect the workings of this form and, in so doing, to deepen understanding of the nature and content of professional development offered by the reading councils. In the end, I return full circle to the theoretical notion of genre and its intersection with the expert presentation. My exploration of the expert presentation makes use of a performative approach to analysis (Bauman and Sherzer 1991; Darnell 1991; Myerhoff 1978; Phillips 1991).

The speaker described here, whom I will call Irene Howard, represents the quintessential council speaker. She is highly sought out as a presenter by councils around the country, and her presentations are considered to be right on target with what members want to hear and how they want that information delivered.

Howard constructs her talk of many small equal pieces, like "beads on a chain" that are loosely linked around an expressive quality. Her talk calls for a high level of emotional response culled from deep identification with teachers' roles and the knowledge that comes with those roles. She is at once terribly humorous and deeply inspiring. As one participant told me, there were not only members who laughed until they cried at her presentation, there were even some who laughed until they wet their pants!

In many ways Howard's presentation reminds one of a religious revival meeting; this should not be surprising, given the council's roots in Protestant practice. Indeed, it is not unusual to find that speakers on the circuit have family ties to evangelical practice. As much as the rhetorical form, this religious feeling is inspired by the comparisons that Howard makes between educational and religious vocation and the evening's spiritual atmosphere of affirmation and support, an atmosphere in which members' spirits are buoyed as they ritually reconfirm their commitment of belief.

The expert presentation, as an opportunity for professional development, is also informative. Howard's presentation provides members with an educational philosophy, instructional strategies, and deeper insight into the meaning of reading as a practice. The content is reflexively linked to the form of presentation.

Expert presentations occur at all levels of council practice. They form the bulk of the one-night offerings of the local councils and, bundled together into a package, the preponderance of offerings at state and national conferences. They are a critical thread binding practice together.

An Evening with Irene Howard

Setting the Context

Six-thirty P.M. on a Tuesday evening in the early fall: I enter the main lobby of the community theater center and spot a long line of women standing at the far end of the room. As I draw closer, I recognize members of the reading council waiting their turn in line at the registration table. I get in line and begin to chat with my neighbors. In front of me is a middle-aged woman in slacks and a red sweater, a teacher in a small town twenty miles from here. She tells me that this is the first reading council event she's ever attended, although she's been a dues-paying member for several years.

Reading council members stream down the stairs of the community center to a lobby area filled with large round tables covered with red tablecloths in a room surrounded by full-length mirrors. At the south end of the room, a book distributor (whom I later learned regularly accompanies Irene Howard on her presentations) is set up and already selling copies of the materials Howard will discuss later in her talk.

Members, who are almost exclusively middle-aged, female, and white, find seats with friends and then make the trek to the dessert table. Over cake and coffee they chat about school and community life, filling the room with animated voices.

Promptly at 7:30, the council president begins the program. She recognizes new members and door prizes are presented. There are reminders about the importance of IRA memberships, and the program chair comes forward to describe upcoming programs. Then, the president presents Irene Howard, the featured speaker. Howard, a state college professor and teacher of many years, is also a past president of a state reading council.

The Presentation

Howard's talk itself consists of four segments that can be plotted like a musical movement: *(a)* the introduction and acknowledgment; *(b)* "molto vivace," a bridge section that quickens the pace; *(c)* "the research"; and, *(d)* "prestissimo," where the tempo is played at its fastest. Each piece builds in a particular way in relationship to the ones before it and after it. The introduction pulls listeners into the world that the speaker would like to create and gets their acceptance of the terms. The second section, molto vivace as I've named it, pushes the tempo faster, offering a hint of the fun to come in the fourth section, the prestissimo. The research section provides what is ostensibly the reason for council participation—the chance to hear "what the research says." In the prestissimo tempo, the mood becomes frantic, leading to a cathartic finale.

Segment 1: Introduction and Acknowledgment

Howard takes the podium. A tall, heavy woman in her middle years with blonde hair and a bright, smiling face, she begins by telling the group to applaud for themselves because she "appreciates so much their coming out after work for this program." She says that she'll start by telling us about herself. "I could say I was the 1968 Miss America. You probably wouldn't remember who that was—just some tall willowy blonde," she mugs. The group laughs for the first, but not the last, time that evening.

"Are there any high school teachers here?" she demands of the audience, looking around intently for a show of hands. "No, no high school teachers here. They don't come without a cash bar." The audience roars at that one.

Howard jokes her way through her biography as a teacher, demonstrating as she does that she has taught at all levels—elementary, middle, high school, and college. She gives the audience evidence of deep understanding of the world of teaching: the drinking habits of high school teachers, the exasperation of working with middle school students, and the clinginess of first graders. She concludes this section by explaining, "I value what you do . . . Teaching is a calling. It's like the priesthood . . . You have to care about the future. It's important work. It's challenging. It's also hard and very draining."

The first segment consists of two linked features, the introduction and the acknowledgment. These two features are linked through the ways Howard develops a deep sense of identification between herself and her audience through showing them how deeply embedded she is in the world of teachers and schools. She builds this picture with bits and pieces of information that only one who has been deeply inside would know—about the alleged drinking habits of high school teachers, the despair that middle grades teachers can feel, and the physical nature of teaching the very young. In a way, she is like a long lost relative finally come home, who, through the stories she knows, stories only someone who had lived there could know, establishes her birthright.

Because she has established her authentic identity in their world, she can then acknowledge them and their work. True acknowledgment, as I learned over my time with the councils, cannot come from outsiders; it is a tribute from those who are inside, from those who know as you know. The more deeply Howard can convey the sense of her insiderness, the more deeply she can acknowledge them. Her listeners know that she has walked in their shoes. She has established the right to anoint them.

From the very first moment, Howard utilizes humor as part of the bond that teachers share among themselves. This is the humor of one who has experienced it all—the vagaries of school administration and the cares of children. Again, this is the laughter of insiders, of people who have lived in this world long enough to be able to say, "What goes around comes around": a symbolic laugh of camaraderie initiated by jokes built from insider knowledge. The laughter, the nodding of heads in agreement, and the raising of hands in answer to questions that Howard shoots at the audience are the beginnings of the physical involvement that she will demand from the audience throughout the evening.

Segment 2: Molto Vivace

After some anecdotes about the draining nature of the job, she shifts topics by saying that she brought some of her favorite books to share with the group.

The first one is a teacher humor book, produced by a teacher who has taken standard proverbs and asked first graders to complete them. Howard shows some of the book's illustrations on an overhead projector. She gives us the first half of a proverb and then asks us to complete it. After we answer, she puts the illustration on the overhead, showing how the first graders completed the proverb. We roar with laughter when we read the first graders' answers.

"People who live in glass houses . . . shouldn't walk around naked."

"Necessity is . . . a trip to K-Mart."

In an instructional aside, Howard urges the audience to design activities for children that leave space for open-ended responses, activities that have no wrong answer.

The molto vivace section serves as a bridge between the highly personal first section and the less personal third section. By shifting tempo, Howard heightens interest. She is gradually building toward the tough fast pace that she will sustain through the finale.

In this section, she also introduces the short segments of activity that will become the primary form of the fourth section (prestissimo). These short segments are, as will also be seen later, framed by homilies or short pieces of instructional information that create the segue to the next segment. In this form, an instructional idea or an introduction to a book is sandwiched between quick transitions. These quick transitions serve as the frames for "the beads," the smaller segments of experience. For instance, here, Howard closes her activity with the proverb book by telling teachers that they should try to incorporate open-ended activities in their own classroom work. This statement provides "the message" or evaluation of the meaning of the short experience with which they have just been involved. Again, she draws heavily on insider knowledge (here the knowledge of the concrete sorts of answers that young children make to metaphor) as the basis for shared humorous moments.

Segment 3: "The Research"

Then Howard shifts topics again, telling the audience that she is now going to show them a list of elements that are part of excellent reading practice in industrialized, English-speaking countries, "countries that are more successful than we are." She explains that these criteria are drawn from research conducted in Australia, New Zealand, and England.

She puts the following transparency on the overhead projector:

"A Well-Balanced Reading Program"
1. Shared Reading
2. Language Experience
3. Guided Reading
4. Independent Reading
5. Reading to Children

Howard works her way through an explanation of each of the five criteria for what she has termed a well-balanced reading program. "In shared reading, everyone in the room is looking at the same text at the same time. Techniques that do this are big books and little books. When the class reads play scripts is another example." She asks if any of her listeners have ever read a poem together with their classes—reading on the board, using a ditto, putting the poem on sentence strips. "Have you sung a song together and read the words together?"

"Grouping," she tells us, "hasn't been good for poor readers. Poor readers need to be in top reading groups. We need more group instruction."

Language experience is "using children's language as part of the classroom reading. It's using their experiences to generate writing and reading."

"Guided reading is the part that we in the U.S. do very well . . . direct instruction, phonics, vocabulary, skills, prediction and comprehension strategies like K-W-L . . . We are very good here . . . but we may spend too much time here. Maybe we've taught too much phonics."

Independent reading is when kids "read for fun . . . not to be tested . . . it's when they read what they want to read."

"Kids aren't reading at home . . . Research tells us the average fifth grade child reads three minutes per day outside of school . . . and they are not reading books then. If we don't provide time in the school day, they won't become fluent readers." She complains that SSR is always the first thing to go when teachers are pressured. "We're too fragmented . . . we have too many things to do."

"If you can teach them to read and write they can do anything . . . so don't worry about the rest," she urges.

"Reading to children is the fifth point," and, Howard says, "it's the most important to me. This is when you nurture their appetite to be a reader. If our students want to read they will be readers. Kids like what they've heard

As Howard makes her points, she demands the audience's participation, most often through humor. At each joke they respond by laughing, answering aloud "ah-ha," and nodding their heads.

"What do you read? . . . Read what you love and what kids respond to."

"Books are friends we visit again and again and again," Howard says intently.

Council members believe that one major purpose of their organization is to provide members with a smorgasbord of ideas, which are based on "the research." This interest in the research may stem in part from the influence of the scientific study of reading, that is, the study of reading as a dimension of educational psychology, a perspective that until recently dominated college reading departments and basal reading textbook publishers (Luke 1988; Monaghan and Saul 1987; Popkewitz 1987; Ruth 1991).

Over the course of my own research, I came to realize that the research of reading councils and research as conceived of in universities are two separate concepts. Council members have great respect for their research and the researchers who produce it. Council members, however, seek different warrants of credibility than researchers. Researchers will want to judge for themselves the design of the study and its assumptions. Council members will listen for reference to the research, as a warrant in and of itself, focusing their attention on the practicality of the classroom suggestions proposed. "Research says," "research has proven time and again," or "innumerable studies prove that" are all considered verifiable warrants from council members' perspective, because for council members, the credibility does not lie in the study referred to, the consistency of the documentation, or the reputation of the researcher as much as it lies in the personal credibility established by the speaker who is passing on that information. The speaker establishes this credibility, as Howard does, through creating an identification between herself and the audience. For this reason, research references in expert presentations made to reading councils may seem extremely limited, vague, and dated to the more critical listener.

Howard prefaces her reference to the research in broad terms, stating that she is going to share with the group a compendium of the very best practices culled from "excellent reading practice in industrialized, English-speaking countries." This attaches the cachet of research to the high-status language arts gurus, many of whom, like Jan Turbill, Brian Cambourne, or Andrea Butler, are from Australia and New Zealand.

What many of her listeners might not have been aware of, and what I only became aware of later in my research, is that in centering her segment on the research around "A Well-Balanced Reading Program," Howard was taking an active part in a dynamic debate currently going on within IRA. The "balanced reading" movement is a backlash against the rising tide of the whole language movement and the growing political strength of its advocates within IRA. Composed of the organization's more traditional members, the balanced reading movement seeks to return the focus of the organization to a more practical orientation. Balanced reading proponents emphasize practical programmatic ideas about "what works," in contrast to whole language advocates, who urge teachers to continually engage in a knowledge-making process in relationship to their practice. The balanced reading movement, like the whole language movement, is highly political in nature. Proponents of this approach have formed a special interest group within IRA and have been active in promoting their ideas at the conference, as have their opponents.

Although her topic is the research, Howard does not let the tone or the tempo of this section lag. Her overhead outlines the five important ideas she wants the audience to listen for, and she quickly works her way through each one, providing basic identifying information, rationale, and some sense of the technique or method associated with each approach. Even though this section is about the research, Howard distinguishes her presentation from what listeners might expect from a more academic presenter. She delivers it in a deeply practical, "what goes around comes around" tone of voice, pointing out how much of this information members already know, how many of the activities they already do, or how easy it would be too simply add on one of these pieces to their current practice.

Here, as throughout the talk, humor is an extremely important component of the process of identification and acknowledgment underway. It continues to serve as a tool to build the sense of identification established at the beginning of the talk, deepening members' sense that they share a special world of experience with the speaker and each other.

Segment 4: Prestissimo

Then she says she brought a couple of her favorite books. The first book she shows is *The Biggest Riddle in the World*. She reads a number of the riddles to the group.

She talks to the group about the ways talking about language and literacy have changed. "For instance, twenty years ago whole language was called integrated language arts," she states. "It's the same thing, it's a different theoretical base, but the same thing." She gives several other examples on this point.

Over the next several minutes, Howard introduces us to the *Homophone Riddle Book*, a book of food jokes called *Belly Laughs*, and a book of tongue twisters. She urges the audience to use riddles, jokes, and tongue twisters with children because they like them, they are nonthreatening, and they integrate the language arts. Humor is sprinkled throughout her book talks, and she receives cheers from the audience when she successfully recites a particularly difficult tongue twister about "Betsy's butter."

Howard tells the group that she looks for books that, "tickle the funny bone, light up kid's eyes, and books that touch hearts by impacting on kids and showing them the power of language."

Demonstrating the power of rhyme, chant, and song, she has the audience participate with her as children would in a first-grade class. "Mary wore a red dress, a red dress. Mary wore a red dress all day long," we chant in unison, substituting names of people and items. When we finish, we're invigorated by our physical efforts.

Building on this theme she engages the audience in the song and hand motions to "The Wheels on the Bus". I look around and see myself surrounded by some seventy middle-aged women singing, "The babies on the bus go Wa-wa-wa, wa-wa-wa . . . the wheels on the bus go round and round," as we roll our hands in circular motions, heads bobbing back and forth as we sing. We end the song enthusiastically. By this point the audience is reaching an ecstatic state.

Howard quickly follows with fractured fairy tales (*The Stinky Cheese Man and Other Stupid Tales*) and then a book about more somber themes (*Wilfred Gordon McDonald Partridge*).

"One of the real virtues of literature is that it takes children to places they may never otherwise get to go . . . Books are ageless and gradeless . . . A good book has a message for everyone."

She picks the tempo up with audience question and answer from an alphabet book, *Q Is for Duck*, which she follows by another book of funny poems, and then shifts to *Finding Buck McHenry* and *Shiloh*, as examples of young adult novels.

"Novels are at the heart of reading," she tells the audience.

She concludes this brief blurb on books for older readers by urging teachers to consider *The Kid's Address Book*, which includes the addresses of numerous famous people to whom they could write. "We hear so much about the reading-writing connection . . . we want the writing to be authentic."

The next selection brings us back to her forte—action and humor. *The Cinderella Chant* is the Cinderella story told as a rap. The audience keeps the beat—clapping, shaking keys, tapping pens against water glasses. Howard reads the rap—blowing into the mike to make the muffled sound that rappers like on their records. The group is laughing so hard that some people are wiping tears from their eyes.

As she begins to make her way toward her conclusion, Howard says, "If we're going to preach to kids about the value of reading we've got to be readers ourselves." She shifts the mood, reading us homespun philosophy from a five-, a twelve-, and a ninety-five-year-old published in the inspirational book *Live and Learn and Pass It On* by H. Jackson Brown. Howard comments on this through a quote from Plato: "Those who dare to teach should never cease to learn."

She shares some of her favorite student writings before concluding.

"What a wonderful service the council serves. I hope you all will come back to other meetings and bring your friends," Howard says, inviting the increased membership that her visits are known to bring to local councils. She mentions that there is a book vendor here, if they want to purchase the books she's introduced.

For her finale, the group sings a familiar children's song—"My Aunt Came Back." It is full of substitutions, physical motion, and complete with a joke ending: "My aunt came back from England and with her brought some *nuts* like you." We clap and laugh heartily at the end as we realize that the joke is on us.

As I make my way up the stairs back to the main lobby, I look down on the heads of the busy mob thronging the book vendor's table. The books are selling so fast that the vendor can hardly keep copies on the table. Council members are busily making out checks for their purchases.

The prestissimo section that completes the presentation is fast in tempo, moving from activity to activity with the aid of quick and effective transitions. In this fourth section, Howard increases audience involvement through activities that require physical participation, of which four of these are in the last section: (a) "Mary Wore a Red Dress"; (b) "The Wheels on the Bus"; (c) "The Cinderella Chant"; and (d) "My Aunt Came Back." Through the use of these four pieces, Howard raises the audience to several emotional peaks, letting them down softly to recover between points—through sudden shifts to more somber moments—but then pushing them back up with quickened action. Although there is much physical action in this section, she controls it. The audience acts in accordance with her commands, not with their own desires.

The range of transitions, the number of activities, and the frequent use of humor are important techniques that Howard employs in this final, dynamic section. The transitions, which add greatly to the sense of intensity, serve a number of functions. In some cases, they serve like Bible verses sprinkled throughout the text of the talk, comforting but moral sayings of great familiarity. An example would be "Books are friends we visit again and again." At other times, the transitions serve as instructional asides, as when she reminds her listeners "We hear so much about the reading and writing connection . . . we want the writing to be authentic." They may also direct the audience toward acknowledgment of their role as teachers. This comes across when she says, "If we're going to preach to kids about the value of reading, we've got to be readers ourselves."

During this presentation, which took no more than an hour, the range of members' activities is astounding. They laugh at jokes, have stories and poems read aloud to them, raise their hands and answer questions, sing, chant, and act out songs. In many ways, Howard recreated the culture of childhood as performed in schools, with council members playing the role of children. Through her performance, school was reinvented and reexperienced.

Interpreting the Expert Presentation as Professional Development

Having walked through the evening's experience, it is now time to turn our sights to the nature of this expert presentation as an example of the professional development of the reading councils. In so doing, there are three intersecting issues to consider: (1) the characteristics that this expert presentation offers as an example of professional development; (2) the instructional information presented, that is, the strategies and materials promoted and the position the speaker takes in regard to the field; and (3) the ethos of reading endorsed by the group.

The Nature of the Experience

The Irene Howard evening is typical of such expert events. Highly ritualized, the format of the evening follows a plan similar to many civic groups. This includes the introduction of officers, announcements about membership and club activities, door prizes, refreshments, and the set presentation. The shared format simplifies expectations for the evening, in that there is not much preparation required by council officers for rituals that are so well defined. Council members can move with ease across civic groups with a fair sense of what to expect as an officer and participant.

While the evening is school focused, it is not school based; that is, it is an occasion for educators from multiple schools and districts across a wide area to come together, rather than a meeting of teachers from within one school. For that reason, the activities of the evening are not tied to the standards or plans of any one particular school or district, rather attention is upon broader issues of general concern to those who identify themselves as reading teachers.

It is also important to note that this is a one-shot deal. The speaker presents ideas that are quick and easy to implement, as opposed to curricular concepts that require lengthy planning and implementation. She offers no follow-up. Tomorrow or the next day she will be giving this same talk to another group of reading teachers. Indeed, this basic talk may serve as her standard presentation to reading council groups for many years to come.

A critical feature of the evening as a professional development experience has to do with the many ways Howard shapes members' sense of identity and allegiance. One way in which she does this is through gender and age. When Howard makes her Miss America joke, she is acknowledging that she, like them, is no longer young and that she is aware she inhabits an older, less perfect body. This gendered acknowledgment draws speaker and audience together.

Another facet of identity and acknowledgment is the importance of the shared knowledge of what it is to be a teacher and to work within the institution of the school. Howard exalts that knowledge and the work of teachers when she refers to teaching as a "calling." In so doing, she draws attention to the religious or vocational overtones that are deeply present in council life (Hansen 1995). She emphasizes the uniqueness of this environment and the problems those who work within it face. She identifies them as an elite corps—specially selected for a difficult but important job. In this she harkens back to the early history of American education and the drive to engage women as part of the teaching force through an integrated appeal to religious values and civic concern (Rothman 1978; Scott 1984).

This notion that the audience is a select elite of believers is unmistakably Protestant, as is the form of the talk and the emphasis on inspiration. This is not surprising given the historical roots of our school system and of educational groups like the reading councils (Tyack 1974).

Allegiance to the organization grows from their shared work world. At the end of the presentation, Howard shifts members' thoughts toward remembering the service that the council provides to them—bringing them together and giving them these kinds of experiences. Howard identifies them, and in that sense ratifies them for the very membership characteristics that they prize most highly—positiveness, good humor, hard work, and a deep sense of caring for young people and reading.

Through her presentation, Howard builds a "liminal space" in which the normal restrictions for teachers do not hold (Turner 1985, 1936).

She does this by warmly inviting the audience in, thus making the presentation space a comfortable place to be. She makes many jokes, laughing hardest at herself. She engages them physically—they nod, wave, tap, clap, sing, chant, and shake their heads. She encourages them to break through the barriers of their normal restraint. Indeed, expert presentations become a type of ritual for members' reexperience of the meaning of their professional beliefs.[1]

The professional development model that Irene Howard presents contrasts significantly with recent calls for changes in professional development, changes which emphasize the study of teachers and learning processes, emphasize individual and organization development and job-embedded experiences, and support long-term, sustained approaches to teacher development (Sparks and Hirsch 1997).

Indeed, the Irene Howard model of training implies not only a different model of professional development, but a different model of schooling, one which presents the school as a discrete unit with set, and fairly unchanging, structure and goals. Teachers in these imagined schools need to add to their tool kit of instructional ideas, but they do not need to rethink the entire notion of the tool kit.

Instructional Content and Context

The central instructional theme of Howard's talk could be described as follows: reading aloud to children is good instructional practice. In support of this point, Howard urged her listeners that when they read aloud to make sure they introduce a variety of books of interest to young people in an entertaining fashion. Practicing what she preached, Howard introduced fourteen different juvenile titles and one adult title to the audience. In the course of the evening, Howard also demonstrated to her listeners a range of techniques for engaging students in the classroom. Her suggestions were both explicit, that is, stated, and implicit, or modeled. Howard presented her views of reading aloud within a particular telling of the story of the discipline of reading/language arts. The books she introduced were later for sale through the offices of a book seller who accompanied Howard on her tour to the councils.

Instructional Content
Howard's explicit suggestions about reading aloud include information about engagement, discussion of genre and form, and discussion of teachers' stance to reading.

Her implicit suggestions are modeled through the techniques with which she engaged the audience. The audience acted out the part of children, experiencing the technique themselves, demonstrating the importance of physical as well as mental engagement in the task. Role reversal also emphasizes the liminal aspects of the experience (Turner 1969).

Viewed as a whole, Howard's instructional suggestions are "thin." They do not stand out nearly as strongly as the fourteen books she introduced in her program nor the entertaining techniques of engagement she employed throughout the evening. Indeed her instructional suggestions are brief and isolated in much the same way that earlier reading instruction with its reading comprehension passages and reading skills practice books made the experience of reading a brief, barely contextualized incident in the school day.

Instructional Context

In setting herself up to talk about what was "most important to me," that is, "reading aloud," Howard described a range of good practices that she sees as composing a comprehensive reading program. Reading aloud is one critical component for such a program. These other elements of a reading program, which she described in the research section of her presentation, include "shared reading," "language experience," "guided reading," and "independent reading." The set coheres, Howard indicated, because of the tested value of the individual items rather than an explicit theory of reading.

In Howard's presentation the list of reading program components are presented as if all were equal items. On closer examination, however, it's possible to distinguish reading aloud, shared reading, language experience, and independent reading as belonging to the category of reading experiences and guided reading serving as an umbrella title for the skills that one might employ in the course of a reading experience. Lacking a distinct theoretical orientation, the distinctions between these groups are flattened to the audience's view.

Howard's instructional ideas are part of her view of the history of reading instruction. As she explains in her presentation, the American educational system excelled in the development of guided reading techniques, that is, techniques for the instruction of reading skills. Over the years, however, and with the help of new research from other English-speaking countries, we have become increasingly aware of the need for a broader range of reading experiences. This call for new and different forms of reading experiences has, most recently, been presented under the banner of whole language. The aim of Howard's program is to present ideas that would support such experiences.

Howard is attentive to the fact that her listeners are struggling mightily to understand the whole language movement that is entering their professional landscape. She assures them that the methods she presents are compatible with a whole language approach and notes, parenthetically, that many of the techniques she is promoting this evening have been present from much earlier on in American schools but with different labels. As many of them live in communities with little or no direct access to these materials, her presentation provides valuable information about instructional materials.

Many whole language advocates would, however, object to leaving it at this. The methods she presented are possible parts of such a program, but she omits the larger, philosophical whole, that is, the comprehensive curricular framework in which to embed them (Edelsky 1992; Goodman 1992).

For whole language advocates, or proponents of a reader-response approach, Howard's suggestions leave little place for the reader as creator of meaning. The materials and activities do not serve as beginning points for inquiry. The experiences they evoke are momentary and fleeting. She provides no discussion of the process of response, no thoughtful way to mediate the immediate experience of the initial reading or practice activity (Rosenblatt 1976).

Critical literacy proponents would wonder about her lack of reflection into the ideological meanings embedded in the texts she presented, and her lack of attention to issues of gender and difference (Knoblauch and Brannon 1993; and Lankshear and McLaren 1993).

Even from a more writerly point of view, Howard does not present the titles with an eye to analysis of the writing except in the most cursory attention to gross details of a genre. The pieces are recommended because they will be personally engaging and present good values, not because they will be examined as models of excellent writing (Prose 1999).

Indeed, the literacy focus presented by Howard is an autonomist one, that is, literacy is seen as a tool separate from its environment rather than a construction embedded in its social contexts (Street 1993). Building from this belief, Howard sees herself presenting a better technology for teachers to use, one that students will respond to with more eagerness than more traditional approaches—but a technology nonetheless. While on the surface Howard's language is compatible with the standards for English/language arts, written with the support of IRA, the underlying structure and thrust of her arguments appear to be in contradiction with that document (National Council of Teachers of English and the International Reading Association 1996).

The discrepancy between Howard's traditional view augmented by selected innovative practices and the critiques of more radical perspectives of such schools of thought as reader-response theory and critical literacy approaches exemplifies the dilemma facing reading council members as they seek to broker traditional and innovative approaches.

The Ethos of Reading

The ethos of reading, by which I mean the broad stream of ideas about reading nourishing council members, circulates throughout Howard's talk in numerous forms. Howard urges teachers to be readers and to read books they love. She talks about books as friends. She emphasizes the need to promote reading to children. She speaks of books that touch souls and literature that can take us to places we've never been before. She characterizes books as ageless and gradeless.

The ways Howard presents notions of reading, the role of reading teachers, and the application of books speak to the ways of thinking about reading that are critical dynamics within council life. In Howard's remarks one sees evidence of the notion that "reading is the foundation of all learning," a statement frequently repeated by members.

Reading, as Howard portrays it, is also a spiritual experience, one that implies transcendence. Members can partake of kind of communion through reading, experiencing this release through the act of reading or through the intervention of books, authors, and ministers of reading, such as Howard.

Reading also becomes a partner in the support of consumer culture as an act and object of promotion. Howard sells books, which is why booksellers are eager to accompany her to her talks, even at locations distant from their businesses. And not only does she sell books, she offers her selling techniques as instructional models to classroom teachers.

The ideas that Howard presents about reading are linked through a hidden logic that makes special sense to insiders. In her presentation, reading appears much like Bourdieu's formulation of practical logic (1977). This logic makes practice appear on the surface to be highly unified but in truth, practical logic exists nowhere, has only a few generative principles, lacks in rigor what it makes up for in simplicity, classifies data from several different standpoints without classifying them in different ways, is indefinitely redundant, and assimilates data comprehensively even when dealing with only one aspect of it.

The reading notion that animates the reading councils is pliant and elastic. Through it, members reiterate their beliefs about reading, restating many fundamental creeds at the same time that they may add new perspectives. In these views, the old and the new are fused. The ethos of reading follows rules, much like those Bourdieu laid out for practice, that is, from a few simple generative principles the world is built.

Conclusions: Genre and the Expert Presentation

Genres provide frames for expression. They are present in every communicative exchange. Members of the reading councils work within genres for the conduct of their business, from the way a business meeting should unfold to the manner in which a reading conference should be organized. These genres of council life are the basis for the expectations members have for their participation in the organization and their interactions with fellow members. Each genre implies particular texts and production, distribution, and consumption practices (Fairclough 1992).

We create meaning through genre as we seek to integrate textual structures within contextual fields. This is a dynamic, active process, in which each instance is historically situated, overlapping with previous meanings that are carried into the present conversation. Because this is so, the "givens" of genre are never homogeneous across speakers and listeners, as they vary based upon context, experiences, skill, etc. Therefore, although the term *genre* implies, to most ears, something that is known, structured, and stable over time, in truth, the use of genre, and the meanings created through this process, are highly variable, emergent, and only provide a momentary semblance of unity. To me, one of the interesting things about the genre of the expert presenter is the way I recognize it across diverse speakers addressing different topics with different audiences.

Speakers manipulate genre in a variety of ways to create expressions that are more appropriate or more true to their needs, concerns, experiences, and expectations for the conversation. Genres vary in their flexibility, that is, the open or closed nature of the form, and in their ability to express individuality or to incorporate other forms or material. They are recognizable by their signature structures, that is, by the situations in which they are employed and the identifying marks of the form, such as the means by which they carry forward content to its completion. Individuals, too, vary in their experiences and abilities to express themselves within a particular genre, as well as in the individual style with which they mark their communications. As Bakhtin says, "Where there is style there is genre" (Bakhtin 1986, 66).

Genres are situated both horizontally and vertically across society. Vertically, particular genres are associated with specific institutions and their activities, such as military activities. Horizontally, genres reach across institutional divides. The genre of a sales exchange is used in many locations, such as a grocery store, a museum, or a conference. Elements of specific genres are borrowed and shared across social life in a particular culture, becoming incorporated in different generic expressions. In this way we nuance, or inflect, one set of speech assumptions with the voices and knowledge of another form. Thus, genres, like language, always exist in a state of dynamic tension in regard to form and meaning, propelled in one direction by centripedal or unifying forces and in another direction by centrifugal or dispersive forces (Bakhtin 1981).

The genre of the expert presenter, offered here in exemplary form, has significance for our understanding of council practice and the meanings of reading that are possible within that practice. These structures define what ideas may or may not enter members' discussion. The ideas that do enter are woven together in characteristic ways. There is great emphasis, as the Howard example shows, on "what works," that is, on the practical, the technical, or the how-to directions. This makes sense, given the instructional hours that teachers must account for in the classroom.

Like the novel, the expert presentation absorbs other genres, in this case incorporating a number of instructional forms, such as book talks, jokes, read-alouds, chants, and other textual activities, into its flexible form. These are probably different activities than one would have seen ten years ago at such a presentation. However, the structure into which they are woven, the expert presentation, has changed little over that time.

As mentioned earlier, the structure of this presentation differs greatly from the essayist talks that one encounters in the university. The expert presentation is loosely structured, providing many small moments of experience, moments that are framed by different kinds of transitions—stories, advice, sayings, etc. The drive is less for an absolute, scientific, provable truth than it is for credibility through empathy and the development of an inspirational moment, one in which the ethos of reading plays a critical role. This structure mirrors members' belief that the organization does not have a philosophy but is, rather, a collection of interests from which members should "pick and choose."

The expert presentation, as it is seen here, closely resembles the Christian revival. This can be seen in members' expectations for the goals of the presentation, as well as in the similarities between Howard's speaking techniques and the techniques of the charismatic Christian ministry. I do not believe that these resemblances are mere coincidence. Council life has deep connections to Protestant practice, and this is yet another example of the implications of these ties.

The ultimate goal of the speaker and the participants is to undergo an intersubjective experience in which they momentarily feel themselves to be one as reading educators. Howard's listeners share a common background and a knowledge of how the story should be told and, in particular, the ways that experts should present themselves. Her deep knowledge of the genre of the expert presentation and the ways that it can be enriched, refilled, and vitalized to create unity across a group make her a valued member of this community.

Note

1 "What is interesting about liminal phenomena for our present purposes is the blend they offer of lowliness and sacredness, of homogeneity and comradeship. We are presented, in such rites, with a "moment in and out of time," and in and out of secular social structure, which reveals, however fleetingly, some recognition (in symbol if not always in language) of a generalized social bond that has ceased to be and has simultaneously yet to be fragmented into a multiplicity of structural ties" (Turner 1969, 96).

Chapter 7

The City of Reading

The annual conference, held in the spring of each year in Springfield, Illinois, is the culmination to the reading councils' calendar year. The production of the annual reading conference is the primary activity and goal of the state reading council.

For this brief space of time those local members attending constitute a short-lived city of reading advocates, filling the sidewalks, restaurants, hotels, and conference facilities of the area in which they have congregated. They room with fellow reading teachers, attend sessions on how to read, what to read, and why reading is important, as well as celebrations of reading and the importance of those who teach and promote reading. Some members will engage in the politics of reading, joining verbal battles for and against specific instructional approaches or forms of reading program organization, while others will campaign for reading leaders of their choice. All will be eager to find good ideas to put into effect in their classrooms and books and other materials that students will enjoy. They will play games about reading, win prizes related to reading, hear jokes about reading, readers, and reading instruction, and sing songs about reading.

> Read on, read on Harvest in the Heartland.
> We love reading books throughout January, February, June, or July.
> Ain't a thing I'd rather do, than read a book.
> So read on, read on harvest time, for me and my books.
> ("Harvest in the Heartland" was sung in a conference session led by a national council leader to the tune of "Shine on Harvest Moon".)

Conference participants will be bathed in a stream of words, images, and symbols portraying reading and messages about it. Reading messages and symbols will be present on the walls of various halls in the form of posters and banners and on the various bags and folders that members receive and even on members' clothing. At the conference, they can truly "live reading" in the fullest way possible.

This once-a-year event brings together local council members from across the state with state and national council leadership, reading luminaries, and commercial vendors in a retreat centering around the notion of reading. Through the conference, the organization's horizontal and vertical structures converge at one time and place. IRC's annual conference is one of many state-level, regional, or higher-level reading conferences that network local members and others together like the reunion of a far-flung clan.

While the overall aim is educational, the commercial element is never far from the surface. In many ways the annual conference is like a gigantic shopping mall of reading wares from textbooks and tradebooks to jewelry and pencils. In addition to the revenue of the exhibit hall, publishers and others also make contributions to support special events and other materials needed to produce the conference, and they will provide special invitations to private entertainments for selected members. The efficacy of state council leaders will be judged, in part, by their ability to barter and negotiate for the resources provided by commercial vendors.

Local councils and their members, even though they may not play an active role in the planning and execution of the state conference, still center their planning for the council year around this event. Councils differ widely in the number of members that participate each year. Some local members attend every year, while other members may attend infrequently, once, or never.

Local council presidents are expected to attend and participate in the annual delegates meeting. For local council presidents and other council officers, the annual meeting is a time to gather information about speakers and programs for future use at the local level. They will also have opportunities to gain a deeper understanding of IRC's and IRA's workings. For some, this will be the stepping-stone to deeper involvement at new levels.

The stories that the two to three thousand attending members bring back from the annual conference about people and activities will continue to be retold at local council meetings over the years. Each conference will be remembered for its own collection of stories, and those stories will impart a special flavor to group's understanding of that era of the organization's history.

For local council members, attending a state or other reading conference is "the payoff" as one member described it to me. This is the reward for the hard work you put in day after day at school working one-on-one and in classrooms with young readers, for taking on extra program duties to support reading achievement, and for volunteering your time to the local council. At the reading conference you are recognized as a professional and a caring educator. Indeed, you are celebrated.

> Mostly the main speakers have been big draws. You know they've had Reggie Routman and Jan Turbill, and they've had lots of big names. And those have been very informative. They're very current in their fields. And I've always done that. And then, just being with other people who talk about what you talk about. It's really nice to get together with people who really think language is important . . . and sometimes you just need a justification or a pat on the back every now and then that says, "Yeh, you are doing the right thing." (Third-grade teacher)

> It's inspiring and refreshing and affirming, and, you know, even if you go and say, "Oh, I do that," you feel kind of good about that. Or if you say, "That's an idea I can use." I find that I like to go to get other ideas, and they have a lot of big name people that do that. And authors and things . . . that's fun . . . I like to go to those things that are well done. I might go this year because my school is supposedly adopting a new reading series, although I don't use the reading series, but don't tell my principal . . . well, I do and I don't . . . but that's a good place to see all the reading series and talk with the sales reps. You can go and look and they give their spiel, and that's kind of neat. (Fifth-grade teacher)

Insiders refer to conferences using the name of the person who was the organizer for that year. In other words, when an IRC member refers to "John's conference" they are speaking of the 1992 conference that then IRC president-elect John Logan oversaw. By the time the 1992 IRC conference rolled around, Logan had spent two years laying the groundwork for this one-time city of reading, a city over which he would preside as mayor.

The purpose of this chapter is to explore how reading conferences serve as opportunities for council members to "live reading" in this temporary city of reading. The questions that concern me here include: How is the experience of the reading conference structured? How do members experience the conference as an aspect of council practice? What are the ways with which the notion of reading serves as a means of connecting individuals and the various communities of practice assembled for the conference?

In order to create this city of reading, conferences dramatically reconfigure members' experience of time and space. Within this shifted configuration, the conference is structured by four significant spheres of activity: (1) informational and inspirational, (2) social and entertainment,

(3) political, and (4) commercial. At the conference, the nature and level of members' participation flows in and around these arenas, constantly nourished by the ethos of reading, that is, a broad range of converging ideas and beliefs that take reading to be their center.

Reading council members are fond of explaining to outsiders how the levels of council practice fit together like a pyramid, each one reflecting the structure and values of the level above it. The symmetry of practice and expectations at local, state, and national levels is a matter of pride. In the reading conference, one can see many of the features of the local council year bundled together to be enacted over a few short days.

The Reading Conference: Displacing Space and Time

Conferences cause displacements in space and time, creating juxtapositions with normal life and engendering a sense that this is something different and special from the routine.

For reading conference members, the conference takes place in a space that is quite different from the one in which they live or work, which for most is the classroom, a unique geographical location and space. Conferences are often held in distant communities, requiring travel and overnight stays. For the short space of the conference, attendees take up residence in a series of hotels clustering the convention center. Conference sessions are held in the auditorium and meeting spaces in the convention center and the ballrooms and meeting rooms in the adjacent hotels. Throughout the day and into the evening, conference attendees wander up and down the halls, searching out rooms for events, stopping to chat with friends, or people gazing during moments of rest on the plush hotel couches.

In moving back and forth between the school spaces in which local councils work and the conference spaces, I have been struck by the physical contrast between these two spaces. This contrast creates a spatial displacement for me as, I must assume, it might do for members. While many of the school spaces I visited were of cinder block construction, the central conference hotels sport elaborate interior decorating schemes with tasteful colors, suggesting an environment of comparative wealth and ease.

Typically, school spaces are decorated with student work and symbols of schools, children, and nationality, from alphabets and teddy bears to the American flag and the little yellow schoolhouse. In school spaces, there are many posters—admonishing (rules and critiques) or promoting (advocating good behavior or ideas). In contrast, hotel spaces are remembered for their bland art and many potted plants. Signs are for direction or advertisements, such as for the restaurant, but these are discrete and few in number.

It is not unusual for conference goers to room with acquaintances—both as an economy and to socialize, creating another displacement in space that contrasts with daily life. During the conference, it is no longer your husband by your side in that double bed but another reading teacher. Instead of coming home to prepare dinner for the family, you find yourself heading out to a restaurant with a gang of newly acquired friends. There are no dirty dishes to do, no beds to make, no clothing to wash, and, hopefully, no papers to grade. The conference disrupts normal expectations of time and responsibility to normal time frames. Participants choose which sessions they will attend out of multiple, simultaneous offerings. They may enter and leave sessions whenever they please and are equally free to go shopping or wander in the exhibits. They are not chained by responsibilities to a class of children whose needs and safety must always be the priority. Ranked relationships, such as those that exist between principal and teacher, are also temporarily abandoned.

The short and intense reconfigurations of space, time, and relationship occurring as a result of the conference create a liminal space for members. This sense of liminality is amplified multiple times by the smaller reconfigurations of space that occur throughout the conference in the many expert presentations and other council activities.

The Four Spheres of Conference Activity

The Inspirational-Informational Sphere

Throughout the conference, members receive information and inspiration about the field of reading from many sources and experiences, but it is particularly concentrated in the small and large sessions of the conference. These sessions are a mosaic of presentations, running the gamut from hands-on teacher demonstrations to talks by reading professors or children's authors and presentations from council leaders. By and large the presentations fall into the category of expert presentations.

The smallest of them take place in out-of-the-way rooms in obscure parts of the conference hotel, while the most important of them will be scheduled for huge ballrooms or conference halls with room to seat hundreds. They may involve a single talking head or in other cases a panel of talking heads. Handouts are appreciated, and overheads are in frequent use, but there are few other visual aids. The expert presentation is, for the most part, an oral experience.

In the introduction to the 1993 IRC State Conference program, the state president outlined the offerings: over 200 sessions, thirty special speakers, and over one hundred exhibitors. There were 211 sessions, to be exact. Of these 211 sessions, 65 were what I came to call "highlighted sessions," that is, they stood out in shaded boxes in the programs designed to catch reader's attention. Presentations by reading council officials and about reading council business were highlighted as were sessions presented by featured speakers, of which there were 39 at this conference. Because featured speakers are invariably connected to a commercial sponsor, although not stated in so many words, events sponsored by a commercial vendor are, thus, given better publicity than those that are not.

Seeking to better understand the scope of the informational arena of the state conference, I conducted a content analysis of the conference program. Working inductively, I developed fourteen category codes to denote the major areas into which conference sessions could be divided. I further subdivided these categories into highlighted and non-highlighted sessions. The results are in table 1.

This tally, while by no means conclusive, does demonstrate the issues that are front and center in council members' minds and the ways that overlapping trends in reading instruction intertwine in council practice. As an example, the reading councils were founded by educators concerned with the specifics of instructional reading strategies and the teaching of impaired readers. One can see from the tally that these interests have been subsumed, in part, by subsequent trends in whole language and writing process approaches.

The outcome of these competing trends is, surprisingly, a new trend—the promotion of authors and books in general. This is a trend that emphasizes trade books but does not exclude textbooks, many of which have been reconfigured in the trade book mode. Presenters at this conference promoted picture books, poems, songs, trade books, fairy tales, drama, and individual authors' works. Where once the emphasis was on specific instructional techniques embedded in a basal reading series, the emphasis now is on the book, genre, or writer.

The bulk of sessions at this conference were directed at teachers of children in grades kindergarten through five, followed by a much smaller number appropriate for teachers of the middle grades and high school. There were a scattering of sessions for teachers of teachers, adult literacy students, and administrators of programs.

Table 1 Analysis of Program Events: IRC 1993 Program Catalog

Presentation Focus	High-lighted	Non-High-lighted	Total
1. IRC Events			
Business mtgs, receptions, speakers re: IRC/IRA	9		9
How-to sessions for IRC publications and *presentations*	1	1	2
Total	**10**	**1**	**11**
2. Promoting Books, Genre, and Authors			
Promoting books in general	3	5	8
Promoting picture books	1	6	7
Promoting particular authors		1	1
Promoting trade books	1	1	2
Promoting nonfiction	1		1
Promoting the use of poems and songs	3	1	4
Promoting use of fairy tales		2	2
Promoting other genres		2	2
Promoting drama		1	1
Author presentations	7	1	8
Total	**16**	**20**	**36**
3. Programmatic Issues			
Policy, national and statewide concerns	3	2	5
Program planning		9	9
Teacher as researcher		4	4
Pre-service education	1	1	2
Assessment	1	8	9
Classroom management	2	1	3
Total	**7**	**25**	**32**
4. Strategies, Tips for Reading Instruction			
Fun strategies, getting through hard times	2	3	5
Specific strategies instruction	3	10	13
Materials as strategies		3	3
Specific reading programs		4	4
General tips	2	1	3
Total	**7**	**21**	**28**
5. Whole Language			
General whole language	4	6	10
Literature instruction (reader-response, *literature groups, etc.*)	2	6	8

Table 1 Continued

Presentation Focus	High-lighted	Non-High-lighted	Total
5. Whole Language (cont.)			
Thematic units		5	5
Reading/writing workshops		2	2
Inquiry		1	1
Total	6	20	26
6. The "Other"			
Gifted and talented	2	3	5
Remedial programming	2	7	9
Multiculturalism/diversity		5	5
Inclusion		1	1
Total	4	16	20
7. Writing			
Beginning writing/writing process	1	4	5
Writing for critical reading	1	3	4
Teaching composition		2	2
Writing across the curriculum	1	2	3
A cross-age writing experience		1	1
Total	3	12	15
8. Feelings			
Humor	1	2	3
Motivation, incentives, decision making		4	4
Adult motivation	3		3
Failure (student)		2	2
Total	4	8	12
9. Parents			
For all parents	2	4	6
Parents of remedial children		4	4
Total	2	8	10
10. Literacy in Other Content Areas			
Math	1	2	3
Science and social studies		2	2
Generally across curriculum		2	2
Fine arts		2	2
Total	1	8	9
11. Computers	2	4	6

Table 1 Continued

Presentation Focus	High-lighted	Non-High-lighted	Total
12. Developmental Areas			
Early childhood	1	2	3
Middle school	1		1
High school		1	1
Total	2	3	5
13. Quality/Meaning of Literacy	1		1
Total of All Sessions	65	146	211

In the conference program index, there are 354 presenters listed. Conference presenters fell into four categories: (1) educators, meaning public school faculty and administrators; (2) university professors; (3) commercially connected speakers (authors, etc.); and (4) other public institutions. Some speakers appeared multiple times on the program, and others only once. Speakers sometimes represented more than one category in their presentation as in the instance when a university professor was sponsored, as a speaker by a publishing company.

Information and inspiration as it is distributed in these sessions is not only a matter of what is presented and by whom but also concerns how it is advertised. Perky, positive, hands-on, practical, and active are words that come to mind when I think about the conference program. Here are some examples of presentation titles and blurbs illustrating this point:

#14 Rickets, Trains, and Skateboards—A Guide to School-Wide Reading Incentive Programs
This session will provide a step-by-step guide to the implementation of a variety of all-school reading incentive programs. Five comprehensive programs will be provided to inspire and create a literature-rich environment within your school. Included will be plans of how to organize, motivate, and follow through each phase of the programs and ideas for implementing these programs.

#20 Teachers + Parents = Partners Promoting Literacy
Research has shown the importance of parental involvement in a child's education. The Parents and Reading Committee has developed workshops and publications designed to promote parent involvement. In this session, we will share

suggested workshop guidelines, parent workshops, and publications for parents of children ranging from preschool through high school.

#28   Whole Language, Cooperative Learning, and Thematic Units: Putting It Together Successfully
Are you having a difficult time using thematic units and cooperative learning within the whole language philosophy? Successful strategies are shared with creative and innovative examples to take back to your classroom. Children's samples will be exhibited with easy-to-follow directions available to the participants.
(From the 1993 IRC Conference program catalogue)

Within these many sessions, one finds many variations and mixtures of the expert presentation genre described in the previous chapter. While sessions may vary considerably from presentation to presentation and speaker to speaker, it would not be inappropriate to assume that presenters at the state conference, like speakers at local council events, will use a positive and cheerful approach, humor will be in abundance, and that many practical and useful ideas for classroom practice will be presented. Good speakers will shy away from ideas and approaches that members will label "theoretical," and they will tailor their talks to follow the "beads on a chain" approach of the expert presentation genre as opposed to a more formal essayist presentation of information. Speakers who do not meet members' notions of good speaking find their audience diminishing over the hour as council members are apt to vote with their feet if they don't like what they hear.

The Social and Entertainment Context

Social events at reading conferences are of both an informal and a formal nature. Informal interactions occur between sessions in the many waiting areas of the conference. Friends greet friends, make plans to eat together, and share information about sessions they enjoyed or speakers to avoid. My field notes from conferences are filled with mentions of these numerous kinds of informal contacts made in the lobbies, restrooms, and halls of these cities of reading. The more people you know and the more deeply invested you are in the reading world, the more numerous such contacts will be and the larger aspect such informal interactions will play in your conference experience.

Rooming together also creates a special kind of fun and social ambiance among council members. In late night gab sessions before the lights go out, friends evaluate conference activities and share gossip about participants, districts, and publishers. Roommates will network for each other, creating introductions to people and activities and, thus, extending each member's opportunities to participate more fully in the social side of the conference. A temporary, but enduring, sort of family social unit is formed by council members who room together with the same group year after year.

In contrast to these informal social meetings, formal entertainment comes in the form of special speaker events, meals or receptions, and honorary events—all of which are distinguished by their highly structured format. An example of such an event would be the young author's banquet at the Illinois State Reading Conference. This is a much anticipated event for which the speaker will be announced well in advance of the conference, and, indeed, the quality or fame of the speaker is considered a major draw for conference participation. Hundreds of council members will attend to hear Newbury prize winners like Lois Lowery or Patricia McLaughlin provide an after-lunch speech. Other formal entertainment might include a late-hour Karaoke party, an organizational birthday party, or a reception for councils achieving Honor Council status.

The elaborateness of the entertainment varies with the level of the conference. Local conferences are less elaborate than state conferences, which are less elaborate than IRA annual meetings. Entertainments run from simple receptions to the media-hip party for IRA members sponsored by Paramount in the Toronto stadium for the 1994 IRA convention.

We leave our dinner with the salespeople from a publishing company about 10:00 P.M. to walk down to the Sky Dome for the Paramount party. In the dome, laser lights play on the ceiling in astrological symbols. We make our way down to the astro turf, at the base of the tiered seats, that stretches green and wide. There are adult games located at various points on the green: a big plastic pillow that you can jump upon in a velcro suit, cages that you get strapped in and then get whirled around. At the far end of the arena is a band on a stage singing clean-cut 60s stuff. A gigantic screen shows us the smiling faces of dancing IRA members wearing the billed hats that were a Paramount giveaway. The two male lead singers gyrate and stomp. Behind them there are three female backup singers in short pink dresses. Suddenly the lights get low, the arena darkens, and fireworks go shooting noisely off toward the ceiling of the dome. There's a whirling sound and a light like a missile speeds out over the heads of the dancers, and another, then red ones, running on wires into the bleachers . . . Before the fireworks started, Paramount ran its logo with clips from Star Trek and Star Trek theme music. (From field notes made at the 1994 IRA convention in Toronto)

The number and elaborateness of events are directly referenced to the amount and kind of financial support that council leaders are able to wrest from commercial supporters. It will vary in relationship to conditions internal to the publishing industry, the strength of ties that council leaders have been able to forge, and the presence or absence of such upcoming events as state reading-adoption decisions.

Conference participants attend reading conferences for professional development, and they see their social activities or the entertainment as supportive of their devotion to their subject.

The Political and Organizational Sphere

The political and organizational sphere of conference life includes those activities dedicated to the reproduction of the organization through the election of officers and decisions related to the structure of the organization and its future policy directions, not to mention the actual running of the conference.

For a smaller but dedicated group of council members, the annual conference is a highly politically charged event, filled with crucial organizational decisions, if not political struggle. Most conference goers blithely pass by this aspect of conference life without a second glance, often unaware that it is constantly surging around them.

Like the social and entertainment sphere of the conference, the political and organizational sphere has both informal and formal components. Informally, lobbying, building constituencies, and negotiating upcoming decisions occur in the lounges, shops, and restaurants of the conference hotels. This activity only becomes visible when you are aware of the players—who they are and what they seek. The more deeply I entered into organizational life, the more these patterns of meetings meant to me.

Reading council members pride themselves on their "roll up your sleeves and get it done" attitude that spurns bickering or arguing, and golden eras of organizational development are ones identified as times when everyone could get along without fighting. And yet, disputes and differences are an ongoing part of organizational life in the reading councils, as in any other organization. During the years when I attended most closely to the Illinois reading councils, political issues of concern included the growing dissatisfaction of the largest state council—the whole language group—with the more conservative and eclectic approach of the larger state organization and rumblings that it might break off to join the Whole Language Umbrella (TAWL groups) or the National Council of Teachers of English (NCTE). There were concerns about the development of a state reading foundation, disputes about the dispersal of funds, and tensions around the selection of leaders.

Political involvement in the reading councils, as anywhere, is not solely disinterested. For some reading council members, participation is an avenue to political power and personal recognition. They relish those fruits of participation and spend long hours of effort to attain them.

Formal political events invariably include the delegates' assembly, at which the successes (although seldom the failures) of the past year are proclaimed by the outgoing president, state officers are elected, bylaws changed, and resolutions passed. Most local members, even officers of local councils, find the proceedings rather dull and often wander out to other events before the meeting is concluded. Members with strong interest in the state organization, however, participate with keen attention to the nuances of the discussion and the significance of the decisions.

Local councils are both the stepping-stone to participation at the state or higher levels and the constant check to that power. Local council presidents play a critical role in influencing local members to attend the delegates' assembly so that a quorum will be present and in taking positions on supporting state leaders who local members will follow. There is much arm-twisting from state leaders to get local leaders to come to the delegates' assembly and much arm-twisting from local leaders to get local members to attend.

The Commercial Sphere

The Exhibit Hall

As I wander through a convention center at a reading conference, I hear numerous repeated statements from an amateur announcer:

> Teachers, there are 110 exhibitors here. There are lots of aisles. Go up and down every aisle. Make sure you visit every one of them.
>
> Stay with us and enjoy the exhibits. There are tables and chairs where you can rest.
>
> For those of you who have just come in, there are 100 exhibits. Make sure you visit them all. (From field notes at a state conference)

I am reminded of both a local county fair and a national radio fund drive. These messages build upon the numerous messages delivered by conference leaders in every session—please visit the exhibits. "This is all they [the exhibitors] ask of you," stated one speaker.

The commercial ties that anchor the conference are concentrated and made visible in the exhibit hall. Gathered within a large convention hall, the exhibits at state conferences are colorful and appealing, and this is even more so at an IRA conference, where months of preparation go into the design of booths and promotional events and items. The biggest booths in the best locations are taken by the most powerful publishing firms. Their banners proudly proclaim who they are, identifying them with brand ideas.

The booths are highly imaginative, often resembling the sets of a play. Actors are often hired to play the roles of storybook or media characters. At the same conference, Paramount used actors dressed up as *Star Trek* characters to promote their reading products. It does catch your attention to round the corner of a display of children's trade books and find yourself face-to-face with Data or the captain!

The exhibit hall is a must-do activity for every conference attendee, regardless of their level of activity in the organization. For some teachers and librarians, the exhibit hall is one of the few opportunities they will have to see a range of resources available in this field. Others are searching out enrichment materials for their classrooms, trade books to supplement the basal reader, strategies to enhance a unit they have used or are planning to use, and instructional aids like posters. Still others dally at the booths of jewelry and clothing embossed, embroidered, and painted with symbols of school or reading, seeking presents for colleagues who were unable to attend.

The routine activity of browsing among the wares is punctuated and enlivened by a variety of promotional activities sponsored by the vendors. Long lines within the aisles often indicate that an author is present at a book signing. Contests and prizes are regularly announced over the loudspeaker, as well as special offers. At the booths, you may be urged to sign up for a drawing.

For many, one of the most enticing aspects of the exhibit hall is the freebies. Freebies come most often in the form of posters or souvenir items like book bags, pencils, novelty items, etc. This part of the conference becomes a friendly contest between conference goers and exhibitors. Conference goers seek to get as many freebies as possible from exhibitors, while expending the least amount of effort on their own part. When friends greet and meet at the exhibit hall, they often exchange information about who is giving away what, what you have to do to get it, and how many are being given away to each person. In the evenings in hotel rooms across the city, members spread out their loot like children coming back from a successful evening of trick-or-treating and decide what stuff is valuable and what is junk, how they will use different kinds of items, and what items they might share. Working the vendors in this way is a time-honored sport for conference attendees, considered one of the enjoyments of living reading in this short-lived city of reading.

The exhibit hall may also serve as a venue for special one-shot promotional events. One conference I attended sponsored a "Midnight Madness" in the exhibit hall. For this event, exhibitors agreed to open their booths in the evening hours following the delegates' meeting. They offered candy or cookies at many booths. This was billed as a major conference activity, and state leaders promoted it each time they spoke. The event itself was nothing more than the booths being open at an hour when they were usually closed, with the hope that participants who might have been tied up in sessions during the day would take this time to visit the commercial booths.

Commercial Ties beyond the Exhibit Hall

In each one of the areas of conference activity—the informational and inspirational, the social and entertainment, and the political—commercial vendors and the resources they possess play an important role in council practice. Featured sessions are sponsored by publishers and others. Receptions and meals are provided by the vendors. All of these grease the wheels for the political business of the conference.

As the reading world shifts and evolves to new currents of thought, this close relationship raises contradictions. Commercial vendors in the reading world mean basal readers and basal reading textbooks have been looked upon as the symbol of traditional reading approaches that are in opposition to whole language approaches. One member described the tension this way:

> [T]hey are still not ready to branch off from that supportive basal reader because of the finances. So, I think there has to be a strong traditional focus there, certainly as evidenced by the role of basal reader publishers. But they've gotten involved in some other things. I think their relationship with U of I has been one of the things that drives them further . . . but I always wonder how much of that gets undone by the publishing companies. You can't have David Pearson holding these research conferences, on the one hand, and then have three times that number all supported by basal readers. It's as if there is a hidden curriculum operating. We will do this [support other reading approaches], but we will do our financing this way. (Interview with longtime state reading leader)

It is important to note that while conferences may look like the primary organizational support, this is not the case at the IRA level, where only about 20 percent of the organizational income comes from conference revenue (interview with Robert Jones, Director of Finance, June 22, 1993). It is important to note, however, that official vendor support is rendered as revenue from rental of booths in the exhibit hall; this may not account for unofficial support through donations to materials and other activities. In state organizations, where the conference is the major activity of the year, unlike the national level where publications, grants, and other income generation activities occur year-round, dependence on vendor revenue may make up a larger portion of the overall budget.

In support of the current system, members insist that vendor participation allows the state organization to keep conference costs down, making it possible for students (future teachers) and teachers from poor districts (lacking any school support for professional development) to attend an event that will provide them with valuable new teaching ideas and access to new materials in their field. In interviews with numerous local members, I heard many stories about the importance of the opportunities that the reading councils provide to members who would otherwise be isolated from collegial interaction.

The Experience of Members

Outsiders and Insiders: Indexing Participation

At the state conference, as in local council practice, members are indexed from outsider to insider status. Conference experiences differ widely among members based upon this status. Table 2 distinguishes what the outsider experience might be in relationship to the different spheres of conference activity versus the insider experience. Those at the outside end of the continuum will be members with closest association to local councils, while those at the inside end of the continuum will be members with closest association to the state and/or national council.

The conference is a time when opportunities for changing membership status open up for many local members, as outsiders seek opportunities for deeper engagement and insiders provide invitations for new kinds of organizational involvement. This movement takes place in many forms. Insiders and outsiders may have chances for relaxed talk while driving to the conference, in meetings at the convention, or in conversation at a formal dinner. A council leader may ask local members to attend the delegates' conference, invite a new member to a private reception, or make introductions between teachers in their district and publishers' representatives in the exhibit hall.

Volunteering at the state conference is a good beginning for members who would like to move up in the ranks. I tried my own hand at this and found myself rubbing shoulders with members from across the state as I passed out registration materials as conference goers arrived and took

Table 2 Outsiders, Insiders, and Conference Participation

Member Level	Information & Inspiration	Commercial	Organization & Political Participation	Social and Entertainment
Organizational Outsiders	Attending sessions is major activity of the conference. Do not make presentations themselves	Wander in the exhibit hall Enjoy handouts and freebies Enjoy seeing reading elites and authors up close Purchase materials for classroom preview Get a personalized sense of the publishers and their work	Little or no vested interest No political participation No responsibility for conference organization or conduct	Participate in exhibit hall entertainment Little participation in special or invited events Enjoy rooming with colleagues from one's school Go out to eat with colleagues from school or eat alone
Organizational Insiders	Attend few sessions as it interferes w/other conference activities May be on presentation circuit in one or more capacities	Personally know and are connected w/various vendors & salespeople Receive invitations to vendors' privately sponsored events Responsible for negotiating vendors' underwriting support	Strong vested interest Multiple forms of political participation Responsible for conference organization and its conduct Negotiate connections between state and national level around the conference (Honor Council, special guests, etc.)	Exhibit hall is place to talk w/friends from across the state Room often w/colleagues from other areas. Attend many special receptions and dinners that are both business and social in nature

luncheon tickets for a featured author event. In these ways movement from local councils to other levels of organizational participation is afforded to members.

Indeed, I learned much about the passage from outsider to insider through reflections on my own journey in the organization, a form of legitimate peripheral participation (Lave and Wenger 1991). Through my research of the organization and participation with members who were insiders, I, too, moved to greater levels of insider status. As I did so, I found the organization more and more inviting and friendly. Where I once dreaded the conferences, afraid that I would know no one and be left standing on the sidelines, I now looked forward to them as opportunities to see friends and catch up on their lives. There were many people whom I recognized in the halls, hotel lobbies, general and small sessions, and receptions. People would smile and wave as I passed, or stop to talk and gossip about the latest council news.

As I experienced this change in my personal level of comfort and acceptance, I simultaneously experienced a change in attitude toward the organization. I was less critical and more protective. I felt that I was laughing with them now, as someone who had more of a family relationship to the issues.

My own experience helped me to understand how it is that many council members experience a great sense of relief at the conference, as if they have come home to family in some way. They enjoy the feeling of being with people who believe, as they do, that reading is the most important thing. "People think you go to these conferences so you can go to new places and see the sights. They don't realize that to me the conference is like a candy shop. Even the bad sessions I like because you're there with people who care about the same issues" (longtime council member and reading consultant).

Participants find great comfort in the opportunities they have to be with and talk with practitioners like themselves, but they also enjoy rubbing shoulders with reading luminaries, such as children's and young adult's authors, reading researchers with name-brand familiarity, and teachers who have become famous for their practice. The conference brings together both the average members and reading celebrities, overturning the normal expectations of daily distinctions, and again emphasizing the liminal nature of the event, where the abnormal becomes normal. Getting to see or meet these stars in person is one of the benefits of conference attendance. Stories of who met whom are discussed in local groups over the years when mention of the state conference arises.

Identity: Teachers—Gender and Eros
Being insider or outsider is one critical dimension of the conference experience, but there are other dimensions that also shape members' individual experiences. Primary among these are their identity as teachers and the gendered and eroticized nature of this identity.

Reading conference participants are identified and referred to almost always as teachers, even when they are not specifically in such roles at this time in their careers. "Teachers" booms a voice out of the loudspeaker in the exhibit hall, speaking to conference goers. Wherever you go for the days of the conference, the implied audience is always teachers, and the tone of speech is always in deference and celebration of that role and its responsibilities. This is a heady atmosphere for a group of people who feel that they receive little recognition for their hard efforts and, indeed, are under the gun of public scrutiny and criticism on many fronts.

While not all conference goers are female, woman are the vast majority of reading council attendees. Indeed, they are present in such great numbers that female rest room facilities in conference facilities are heavily strained and the waits to use the lavatories between sessions may be quite long, while male facilities are barely used. At one IRC conference, I heard a young waitress, looking around the restaurant in which she worked and commenting on the large numbers of women, state, "This is weird."

The experience of the conference is not only highly gendered, but also distinctly eroticized. Sexuality is an aroma that wafts through halls of the conference. It is present in the crushes and crush-like behavior that the female members often have on reading experts and authors of children's and young adult's books. It is referenced in the T-shirts with messages about teachers as lovers. A negative issue in daily school life, sexuality playfully resurfaces in the carnivalesque atmosphere of the reading conference (Bakhtin 1984)

One longtime member described the distant infatuation she had for a male IRA leader long active in the organization. She purchased tapes of his speeches and would play them as she drove to and from work, thrilling at the sound of his voice. When the creator of the tapes was pointed out to me, I have to admit that I had trouble rectifying the reality of this aged gentleman with the image of the husky-voiced swain that accompanied this council member on her drives to school with narrations on the importance of reading and the best ways to teach reading.

This was not an unhappily married woman, but someone for whom a piece of "living reading" was a little bit of romantic indulgence. Loving her family and teaching life, she enlivened it with this reminder of the heady days of the conference, so different from her day-to-day life. Protesting allegations from a fellow conference goer that this fellow's version of reading issues is a form of reading lite, she said; "This is just what people in this group want. He inspires you and gives you a little information." At the conference such fantasies can be indulged safely at a distance.

Conclusions

Reading is the notion that brings these various people and communities together each year, and yet the meaning of this term and the purpose of the organization varies considerably across individuals and groups. This is as true at the local level as it is at the state. For members of the old school, reading may be about helping nonreaders and the knowledge of specific strategies for these students. Other members may believe that reading is about the full, imaginative development of the child. For some, participation is an avenue for richer professional opportunities beyond the limits of their local district position. Reading, in these cases, means job promotion. For others, it is a chance to leverage new policies for local and state resources—a high-stakes political battle. For the vendors who attend, conference attendees are the key market for school reading materials, but to sell their materials they must position themselves appropriately in relationship to these multiple meanings about reading.

At the conference, notions of reading weave throughout the four domains of activity: informational and inspirational, social and entertainment, political, and commercial. Viewed from a distance, the whole appears cohesive, but up close cracks, seams, and fissures in the surface are visible. These rents in the fabric are inevitable as reading is a constantly moving target used to absorb or respond to numerous perspectives.

For individual council members and the communities of practice drawn together around the conference, reading serves as a "boundary object." As a boundary object, reading provides the glue to hold together the numerous cities of reading that spring up over the year in the form of state, regional, and national/international conferences of reading teachers and their affiliates.

> This is an analytic concept of those scientific objects which both inhabit several intersecting social worlds . . . and satisfy the informational requirements of each of them. Boundary objects are objects, which are both plastic enough to adapt to local needs and the constraints of the several parties employing them, yet robust enough to maintain a common identity across sites. They are weakly structured in common use, and become strongly structured in individual-site use. These objects may be abstract or concrete. They have different meanings in different social worlds but their structure is common enough to more than one world to make them recognizable, a means of translation. The creation and management of boundary objects is a key process in developing and maintaining coherence across intersecting social worlds. (Star and Grieseman, 1989, 393)

Star and Grieseman define boundary objects as translation mechanisms that operate to connect diverse social worlds. As this study of the reading councils demonstrates, however, while boundary objects connect ideas across individuals and groups, I would also contend that they are a mechanism for translating within an individual, across the various communities of thought that inhabit our psyches and that we must navigate to develop a fascimile of intellectual coherence.

It is these two notions—the inter and intra use of boundary objects—that are behind what it is to "live reading." Thus, teachers connect their day-to-day classroom life—from organizing reading groups to grading papers—and the skills they need to conduct this work to their identity as a teacher, and that identity is grounded in the idea of reading. They symbolize this choice through clothing they wear (vests showing books on a shelf, sweatshirts extolling reading) and posters they display in their classroom (sports stars in rocking chairs reading books). They position this identity in the larger scheme of things with the use of the notion of reading. Thus, it is not strange to mix notions of religion and vocation with ideas about reading (i.e., teaching reading is a calling for which only some are called).

For council members, reading is one of the ways by which they bind the parts together and defend the combination to others. To be a reading teacher draws across multiple parts of one's internal life and connects one in a range of ways to diverse external communities of practice. The reading councils are a means of focusing those many internal and external points of translation. Cities of reading in which one can fully live reading allow for the temporary fusing of the internal and external worlds and, thus, the intermingling of multiple communities of practice.

Part III

DISCOURSE, PRACTICE, AND IMPLICATIONS

Chapter 8

The Spirituality of Reading

In 1994, when the IRC conference theme was "the magic of literacy," the program offered this opening message to readers:

Celebrate "The Magic of Literacy"
Have you ever thought how very small a measure of time and space one person's life by itself can be? Only three score year and ten, the prophet said; and how many years is it that men have been living and doing while the earth has gone rolling on? Only one room, one house, one town, one country, to live in—or so it is for the most of us; and how many miles is it of sea and land that is given to men to roam? Why, then, what little creatures we are in all these years of time and miles of space! Could we but travel down the road of yesterdays, and wander round this world, and back against [sic], then it might be that we should understand our own small part in this great society.

"Oh, but," you say, "we cannot; so what a foolish wish!"

Yet listen. A little voice is calling you, or is it only the rustling of paper and the idle turning of leaves? It seems to say—

"I will carry you back the road of yesterdays. Come, read with me!" Author Unknown (Illinois Reading Council 1994c, 4)

In this passage, people are depicted as vulnerable, short-lived creatures against a vast landscape of time and space. This temporal and spatial landscape incorporates the historical, the contemporary, and the future—of this earth and beyond. The writer hypothesizes that we could be stronger and more fortified if we had access to the experiences of other people—and we do, with reading as the means by which we can project ourselves into their lives and gain these experiences.

The opening of the passage ties closely to Protestant notions, the concern with human frailty and the search for fulfillment in this life. Indeed, it even includes a reference to "the prophet." The ideas discussed here, however, also suggest notions of magic—with their sense of other worlds and other times and speculation about human ability to enter other realms. We realize this in the next instance when the reader receives an answer from a vague "other," an anthropomorphized book—a voice representing either the book itself or a character speaking through a book. This voice is a magical device that bids the reader/council member entry into a magical world. The eeriness emoted by "the rustling of paper or the turning of leaves," signals the employment of this device. Magic, as readers of fantasy fiction know, can often be overlooked—as it can appear to resemble natural physical events, particularly at its moment of initiation. Is the voice calling or is it not, is the voice saying it will carry you back to yesteryear or is it only the sound of the wind?

This passage introduces many of the elements of what I have dubbed the spirituality of reading, a discourse about reading that permeates the practice of the reading councils. The discourse of the spirituality of reading, like the genre of the expert presenter, is a cultural and linguistic resource that threads across reading councils and connects them to other overlapping communities of practice.

Prime characteristics of this discourse of the spirituality of reading include: (a) attention to a broad range of concerns that our culture identifies as spiritual; (b) a belief that the discourse itself will serve as a vehicle for spiritual fulfillment; (c) the interdependence of this discourse with other discourses or communities of practice concerned with spiritual issues, particularly those of the Protestant religion and of magic; (d) the portrayal of things related to reading (the act of reading, reading materials, reading teachers, and reading council practice) as spiritually transformative; and (e) the connections drawn between liminal elements and reading, establishing the distortion of time and space and the special assignment of symbolic meaning as aspects of the spirituality of reading (Turner 1986).

As the term *spiritual* implies, the discourse of the spirituality of reading addresses those myriad of questions that ascribe to the spiritual realm: What is the meaning of life? What is the potential that our lives could find? It seeks answers for the unknown and provides salve for what seems beyond our control. It serves as a way to broker the tension between duty and pleasure. Through spiritual outlets we seek affirmation of ourselves as spiritual beings and some assignment of meaning to the grind of our daily lives. The spiritual realm addresses the values and significance of the ways in which we organize communal life and the symbols and rituals through which we sustain community. The discourse of the spirituality of reading seeks to answer spiritual concerns through the act, belief, teaching, or promotion of reading.

Council members use the discourse of the spirituality of reading as a means of expressing notions about reading *and* as a means of experiencing spiritual fulfillment. That is, they come to meetings with the hope that they will be inspired, renewed, refreshed, and reaffirmed. Through participation in council events, they can leave their burdens behind, or at least return to them with new energy. These desires cannot be met by information alone. Thus, while they proclaim that disseminating research-based information on reading is a primary goal of the group, in reality, they direct less attention to that purpose than to aspects of spiritual fulfillment through reading. The discourse of spirituality reassures members that the commitments they make to the profession are meaningful, and that their work is beneficial and contributes to some larger good.

This discourse, like all discourse, exists interdependently among other discourses and communities of practice, in particular those we identify in our society as concerned with issues of spirituality. In the reading councils, the discourse of the spirituality of reading draws most heavily upon the world of American Protestantism. This is a world that comes replete with numerous structures, genres, symbols, roles, and texts. Next in importance as a resource for the discourse of the spirituality of reading is the world of fantastical magic, which also comes replete with texts, roles, symbols, etc.

A critical element of most spiritual systems is concern with the transformative, and the discourse of the spirituality of reading is no exception. A spiritual transformation can include a change in mental attitude, the acceptance of a new belief, participation in a new experience, or the experience of a different reality through distortion of time and space. On a more fantastical level, transformation can mean that one is transported to another time and place or can perform feats that would have been impossible under normal circumstances. In the discourse of the spirituality of reading, books, reading, and reading teachers all have the potential to instigate spiritual transformations in different ways through presence, activity, or intervention. Although transformation can occur through many things—the act of reading, the presence of books, the act of dreaming, the assistance of a teacher, or the support of the reading councils—each transformation implies the restorative power of "reading."

Spirituality and its transformations occur in special liminal zones that distort the daily realities of time and space. In such zones, the insights one finds are spiritual in nature, that is, they are deeper and finer than what one usually encounters in day-to-day life. By distorting time, reading creates a liminal zone. Reading and books are also symbolic of this liminal zone. The discourse of the spirituality of reading exists in council practice where these distortions are found.

My interest in this chapter is to explore the contents that compose this discourse and to demonstrate how spirituality and reading mutually constitute each other through council practice. By mixing spirituality and reading in the ways they do, council practice, which names reading as the center of its world, becomes a spiritual practice. By clarifying the nature of this discourse, I mean to make clear the very particular and situated ways in which members come to "live reading" and to show why it is that reading means so much more to council members than simply the act of deciphering text.

For these reasons, I am particularly interested in the ways that this discourse is positioned at the intersection among a number of different communities of practice. Through the examination of the discourse of the spirituality of reading, I hope to give the reader a sense of the ways that communities of practice interconnect through the shared uses of various linguistic and symbolic resources.

As Fairclough states, discourse is "a particular way of constructing a subject-matter" and thus creates ways of doing, being, and thinking about the subject (1992, 127–28). Thus, the spirituality of reading is a specific framework for understanding the meaning of reading. Like Foucault, I believe the discourse to be composed of statements that are positioned in relationship to "institutions, economic and social processes, behavioral patterns, systems of norms, techniques, types of classification, and modes of characterization" (1972, 45). Discourse itself emerges from among these relationships. Through their performance, objects of knowledge are located, subjects' identities emerge, and objects and ideas come to hold symbolic value.

In this chapter, the issues surrounding the spirituality of reading serve as a springboard for getting at notions of discourse, and, vice versa, notions of discourse serve as a means of getting at what the spirituality of reading means.

In eclectic fashion, I look at three groups of examples in which traces of the discourse of the spirituality of reading can be strongly discerned. In the first instance, I examine selected roles that members play in relationship to literacy issues. In the second, I examine the ways the book serves as a major symbolic icon. In the third, I consider the ways that reading, reading teachers, and/or the reading councils are seen as transformative practice.

None of the examples are exhaustive or exclusive. It is important to remember that new instances and forms of the spirituality of reading are always emergent. That is to say that roles, symbols, and transformative practices are only one among numerous lenses we might don to view this issue. In that sense, it truly makes more sense to search for traces and to assume that what evidence one has about the discourse will always be partial and dated. In addition, nothing about a discourse appears in an idealized, pure form, because the discourse itself is a relationship cobbled together among various institutions and their communities of practice; it is a thing of borrowings and indications. How these items are stitched together reflects the intertextual relationships among communities of practice.

Roles

Discourses circumscribe roles for speakers. Within the reading councils there are numerous roles—the grassroots members, the local leadership, the reading gurus that travel "the circuit," and the authors. Each one has different options for speaking about reading. In crafting the roles they assume, council members or participants draw upon the resources available to them through their access to overlapping communities of practice. Notions about reading are central to all aspects of these roles.

In this section, I look at two fieldwork events that illustrate facets of the use of roles as a feature of the discourse of reading as spirituality.

Testifying for Reading

In the following example of role crafting, I present young-adult book author Gary Hatchett testifying for reading, using a form that can be heard at all levels within council practice. In offering this testimonial, Hatchett draws heavily upon Christian forms, making strong reference to the transformative nature of reading as a practice.

It is 7:30 A.M. on a sunny spring day in Toronto, Canada, during the 1994 IRA convention. I am attending a breakfast buffet sponsored by Bantam, Doubleday, and Dell for their all-time favorite young-adult author, Gary Paulsen. Paulsen, author of *Hatchett*, which the promotional people tell us is the best-selling young-adult book of our time, comes briskly to the podium. My neighbor, a young adult librarian, is about to hyperventilate from the excitement of seeing Paulsen in the flesh because, as she willingly admits, she has a terrible crush on him.

Paulsen's speech centers on the telling of three literacy incidents in his own life. [I omitted the first two for brevity's sake; the third speaks most clearly to teacher's roles.]

The third literacy incident is a page from Paulsen's own childhood. "My folks were the town drunks," he recounts. "I flunked everything." As a young teenager he was selling newspapers in bars at night to keep body and soul together. One evening he went into the library to get warm, and the librarian gave him a card. He was astonished by her act, but began to take books home and hide in the basement to read them when his parents were drunk. He continued to hide and read for the next one and one-half years.

Paulsen concludes, "Everything I've become comes from that one time with that one librarian who turned me on to reading." He explains to the audience that humans are the one species that have chosen to store their knowledge in print, "Everything we are is locked up in print. All the things we know—science, love, hate. If you don't read, that's lost . . . Reading is incredibly important," he tells the group, complaining that our world is "going down the toilet and a lot of that is because we've neglected reading."

On that morning in Toronto, Paulsen was speaking to the converted. Many people in that audience had heard him speak before and knew of the story of his own entry into literacy. Indeed, they went to hear him retell it, because in the retelling there was affirmation of their own belief in literacy's ability to save lives and educators' role in extending that life jacket to the nonreader. It is a story that speaks to the passion they share for the teaching of reading. It invests that passion with symbolic meaning. Reading affirms the value of the individual, and teachers affirm that value for young people when they make special efforts to reach out to them.

Paulsen's testimonial includes several overlapping notions of reading— the belief that reading is fundamental to learning, that it is fundamental to humanity, and that it is the key to spiritual and species survival. At the same time that he uses the Christian form of testimonial, he also draws upon our knowledge of this testimonial as part of recovery stories told in such groups as Alcoholics Anonymous. These are some of the very obvious ways that genre, communities of practice, and discourse are intertextually linked here through council practice.

As a star author, Paulsen plays a special role within Protestant practice as it applies to council life. He is both saved sinner and itinerant preacher. Other roles that council life borrows include those of minister (such as Howard occupies), Protestant nun or female lay worker, saints, infidels, and missionaries. Paulsen also defines roles for reading teachers or their affiliates, in this case, the librarian.

The New Elders

In contrast to the first fieldwork incident above describing the role of testifying for reading, in the next section, reading teachers take on the role of "the new elders."

One of the councils I studied organized a reading carnival, which starred a professional storyteller. The storyteller, a large man with a bushy beard

who played a guitar, had a soft tenor voice. At the beginning of his performance, the storyteller spoke of the special role that belongs to the new
elders—teachers, librarians, and storytellers—who are now responsible
for passing on stories and their heritage to children because no one else
takes responsibility for such learning.

The storyteller, a folklore specialist with knowledge of many different
cultures and their stories, equated council members' cultural roles to the
elder role as it is described in traditional tribal cultures. An elder has long
familiarity with his or her own culture and is in a position to assist in its
preservation, transmission, and interpretation. Elders are valued members of their culture; they work with the young, as do teachers. Their
work has spiritual value because it addresses questions of the spiritual
realm. Elders are often brokers of sorts with the spiritual world, or inter-
preters of their community's spiritual needs or losses.

"New elders" is a singularly appropriate term to describe the ways
council members see their responsibility to those they serve, and it provides a fitting image for the roles implied for teachers within this discourse. It rings true with the way I have come to believe that members
view themselves and their world, that is, that their work, more than just
labor, is a special calling.

Teaching, then, is service one enters when one is called (Hansen 1995).
Teachers, despite difficult work conditions they may face in their jobs and
their failure to garner the respect they feel that they deserve, work on a
higher plane than those in other professions, and that higher plane is
tinged with the spiritual and the moral. Teachers deal with children from
increasingly difficult situations, children who lack the parental support
that should provide them with moral guidance. Thus, the new elders must
step in to fill this role with the aid of reading. Through the development of
reading skills and the promotion of reading, the new elders provide young
people with opportunities for moral development, social integration, and
a promising future.

Characteristic of the notion of discourse is the way that it defines roles
and subjectivities. Because council members channel many of their expressions about reading through the discourse of the spirituality of reading, members and other participants craft their roles within the parameters of this discourse. In the two examples here, speakers demonstrate
the intertextual quality of this discourse (Bakhtin 1981). Hatchett testifies
for reading, serving as fallen sinner, now revived. He speaks about reading through the form of the Christian testimonial, a form sanctified by
Protestant practice. The storyteller, on the other hand, presents a meta-

phor for council members' participation from outside the boundaries of Christian life, but one that equally imbues their work and the meaning of reading with spiritual significance and status. In their presentations, both Hatchett and the storyteller perform and teach roles in which spirituality and reading intertwine to constitute a specific view of the world.

The Book: A Symbolic Center

Shifting from roles, another way of approaching discursive practice is through an examination of the special symbols associated with the discourse. While numerous symbols figure in council practice, the book has particularly special spiritual meaning. Books deliver the moral messages that one needs to hear to feed the soul. They are symbols and sources of salvation.

The symbolic attribute of books lends itself well to visual representation. Local council newsletters provide ample evidence of this. In these newsletters, books are presented as realistic illustrations. Someone is reading or holding a book, or books are included as part of a background. Books are also presented in animated form, such as a marching line of anthropomorphized books with smiling faces on their spines. These anthropomorphized volumes are always happy, never angry. After all, they are our friends. Finally, books form part of logos for various organizations or projects, indicating that literacy is the essence of the group's work. It is the book, and the book alone, that plays such a symbolic role in council iconography. In this role, the book signifies multiple meanings related to literacy. It is imbued with all the values that council members attribute to reading.

It is important to note here that some of the symbolic pictures of books are received by members and others are created by them. Received pictures consist in large part of prefab art from cutout books or computer picture files created by commercial publishers of different sorts.

Talk of the book and symbolic reference to it are reflected back to council members in various ways. Howard's presentation made numerous references to books as ageless and gradeless, as our friends, as devices that can transport one to other places. These are standard ways of referring to books within the councils. They place Irene Howard squarely within the spirituality of reading discourse.

Members' concern with the book as symbolic of the discourses regarding reading is also reflected back to them by publishers. At various conferences, publishers not only exhibit books, but also provide numerous portrayals of books, developing staged book scenes of various sorts. According to sales representatives, many of the largest and most elaborate scenes have been a year in the planning. For instance, at the 1994 IRA conference in Toronto, the Harcourt Brace exhibit space was set off by several gigantic props, replicas of the latest editions of their basal reader program. These props were taller than the average person. Placed like books, standing partially open on the floor, each one created sheltered merchandise display spaces for the sales crew. People strolling through that part of the exhibit area had the sense that they were walking right into a book. In that way, the Harcourt Brace exhibit mimicked the sense of liminality, that is, the distortion of time and space that is also such an important part of the discourse of reading as spirituality. Many other publishers created comparable exhibits.

In many ways, books have a unifying function, something like the communal wafer and wine. They are concrete symbols of a complex of densely woven concepts that encompass a vast worldview. Communion is about the transformation of Christ's body into a symbol that all can partake of. Communion, thus, is a unifying force, bringing people together to celebrate their shared beliefs. This sweet and bitter ritual combines salvation, through Christ's sacrifice, and repentance, our acknowledgment of our sins and unworthiness. Books are symbolic of the act of reading, which, as Hatchett described earlier, can redeem individuals from sin. Reading can lead one away from self-destructive behaviors through providing hope, better role models, or escape from unhappy situations. One can literally be saved through reading, and books are the symbol of that redemption.

Like the communal wafer and wine, books provide a unifying symbolic center for the practice of reading. Situated among discursive practices infused with Christian religious meaning and symbolism, the book, too, absorbs this incense.

Transformative Practice

Finally, a third way to illustrate the discourse of the spirituality of reading is through looking at incidents of council practice as transformative practice. The first example is lighthearted. Drawn from a local council newsletter, it is a letter from the president to the members, using the metaphor of "the magic of literacy" as a means of promoting the year's upcoming events. This text draws deeply upon the world of magic—its notions, gimmicks, genres, etc. The message is that the reading councils have the magic that can transform teachers' reading practice. The second example strikes a more serious note, focusing on the notion of the dream as portrayed in council life. It draws upon two vignettes, the first is a talk by the then IRA president, Doris Roettger, and the second is from the talk of an IRA official at a state leadership meeting.

We've Got the Magic

The world of fantastical magic enters reading council practice with its own set of conventions and notions, and many texts provide us with our knowledge of these conventions and notions. Teachers live in close contact with children's literature, within which fantasy is an extremely important genre. The genre of fantasy includes fairy tales, folklore, classical fantasy from writers such as E. Nesbitt, C. S. Lewis, and Edgar Eager and features newer fantasy classics like the Harry Potter books. From this mixture of fantasy worlds, the discourse of the spirituality of reading draws many images. For instance, magical moments, like spiritual moments, are identified and separated from ordinary experience in a variety of ways. Magic often requires a magical device of some sort, often provided by the book, that is, reading the book is the portal itself. Magic may come in the guise of magical creatures—witches, goblins, and princesses.

While many would frown on the inclusion of magic as part of a discussion of spirituality, there are important parallels between the two that argue here for magic's inclusion as an aspect of spirituality. Magic deals with many of the issues raised earlier that are at the heart of what we consider to be spiritual—the significance of our present lives and the potential for our future lives, the issues of good and evil, and the methods for improving one's lot. Like Protestant practice, magic brings with it a comprehensive world that includes roles, subjective positions, symbols, and genres of presentation.

A council president uses the idea of magic in her members' newsletter:

> Fall is definitely in the air and the coming holiday reminds us of magic. Thoughts of witches and goblins, harvest moons and Indian summer add to the excitement of the season. The school year flies by so rapidly that it seems as if a magician spins the hand of the clock so quickly thus reminding us of how quickly time passes and how important it is to make the most of every minute we have to teach our students. The Raven River Reading Council hopes to help you make the most of your time by providing some magic wands to bring ideas for magically increasing the effectiveness of your teaching.
>
> Come share in the fun of our Reading Jamboree at Raven River High School on October 1. Not only will you hear Kit Thompson, a delightful storyteller, but

you will have the opportunity to share what your students are doing and learn about what other teachers and students are doing in their classrooms. We hope you will then plan to hop back on our magic carpet and attend our local reading conference at Raven River High School on November 5. Darla Sanders is a nationally known speaker with many ideas and thoughts for you to reflect upon and hopefully incorporate into your teaching as you magically cast a spell on your students. The day will also be enhanced by many small group sessions that promise to help bring enchantment to your classroom. Plan to make your October dazzling as you explore and share the magic of reading.

In this example, the idea of magic is woven together with the school's (and the reading council's) annual calendar as the special atmosphere of magic is evoked through mention of Halloween. The council is depicted as being able to provide magical help to teachers through the presentations and services it offers members. Through the powers conferred by council participation, members will gain magic capable of enchanting their classrooms. Popular cultural symbols of magical beings and the artifacts by which magic is crafted are important here, from witches and goblins to magic wands and carpets, adding cachet to the description.

Reading, in this sense of magical, puts one in a ludic, dreamlike state. It can ferry one to other worlds. Teachers have magical devices to help one to acquire literacy, and teachers serve as the intermediaries to help young readers reach these other worlds. Reading is both vehicle and location from this perspective.

The Bridge of Dreams

In council life, the dream serves as a bridge between reality and another, better world. By its transformational power, the dream is a way to reach a better world. The dream of a better world embraces a world where everyone can read, a world where the council's goals are achieved, and a world where schools have the requisites to produce successful readers. As a symbol, the dream, positioned between magical and Christian discourses, straddles the popular and the religious.

Doris Roettger, a former IRA president, spoke of dreams in her presentation at the 1994 Midwest Regional Reading Conference.

Roettger is tall, very well groomed. She is wearing a green blazer and has a heavy, molded gold necklace around her neck. She is talking her way through a list on an overhead. She talks about the importance of "parent involvement." The necessity of "developing an action plan," and how important it is to "give yourself time to learn." The last two items on the list are "radiate energy, joy, and upness" and "dust off your dreams."

"We all had dreams when we started. We had 20-20 vision. We would help everyone . . . Somehow, our dreams get put in our pockets."

She places a poem by Langston Hughes on the overhead:

Hold fast to your dreams
For if dreams die
Life is a broken-winged bird
That cannot fly . . .

"Help your kids dream so they can reach their potential as readers," says Roettger, finishing her speech. (From Regional Conference field notes)

At the annual IRC state leadership meeting a visiting IRA official closed his talk with words about dreams. He read the preamble to the IRA goals; it talks about dreams and vision. Then he mentioned the words of a song from the musical "South Pacific"—"If you don't have dreams, how can they ever come true?" He closed with, "I hope today you'll start to dream."

Talk of dreams includes an element of past, present, and future. There is nostalgia or concern for dreams generated in the past, particularly during youth, and these are seen to hold special power. However, there is also a belief that the generation of dreams can occur at any time in our life and can be a powerful means of effecting a different future. Indeed, dreams can be the bridge by which you reach a desired future.

Dreams are associated with a positive attitude toward life, the kind of attitude that will generate success in one's endeavors. The teacher's role is to assist students to dream so that they will be able to enter a better world. Council members' role is to dream so that they and their organization will be able to enter these Elysian fields of reading.

These discourses evoke the idea of "here," the reality in which we exist and "there," the imagined world which we may enter or visit with assistance. This imagined world contains the notion of what I would label "the land of reading." Time flows around and through this land in different ways than it does in our usual reality, and for that reason one must be careful to distinguish between the world of our usual reality and that of the land of reading. Time "on the other side" is not linear, narrowly parceled, or morally judgmental. It is easy, therefore, to become lost, oblivious to time, as one does when immersed in a good book, which is a primary means of entering this other reality. When entering this world through books and/or reading, one can travel with ease between vastly different periods of time and the ideas they encompass. Dream time, like dream space, is inexact, marking out chronological territories within which readers can act.

Disparate as these two examples seem, one about magic and reading and the other about reading as a bridge of dreams, they both powerfully depict the transformative nature of reading and the meaning of transformation within the practice of the councils. In the first example, council participation gives one access to magical tools that then make it possible to transform one's practice and the lives and minds of one's students. In the second example, through the employment of dreaming, one can also transform one's own practice or that of others through helping them to dream.

Conclusions

The spirituality of reading is a broad, encompassing term for ways of thinking, talking, and being, ways that circulate around and through notions of reading within reading council practice. The set of eclectic examples presented above offers different angles from which to get at aspects of this particular discourse.

As these examples demonstrate, the discourse of the spirituality of reading is pervasive in council practice. It is present on multiple levels within the organization, from the local to the national. In any given situation it can also be present in the symbol of a book, the role a speaker takes, or the images that listeners or readers receive. The spirituality of reading is highly reflexive. The genres, images, and roles that emerge from within the councils are often reflected back to the councils from without and then refracted outward again. While this discourse is not exclusive to the reading councils, it is closely identified with them; and the form it takes within the councils is a uniquely identifiable signature of council practice.

Reading councils as a community of practice overlap with other communities of practice in a meaningful manner. Council practice provides many examples of the intertextual weaving process that connects multiple discursive worlds. For example, author Gary Paulsen testifies for reading in much the same way that an alcoholic performs at a meeting of Alcoholics Anonymous, a group with Protestant roots. Other speakers draw upon poetry or musical scores to describe the transformative power of dreams as applied to reading practice. It is not only the forms that are drawn into the reading councils, but also the ideas, as when Paulsen depicts reading as salvation and reading teachers as saviors.

The discourse of the spirituality of reading is highly elastic. At its center is a vague notion of spirituality and the questions that one addresses in this realm. It harbors an eclectic set of ideas under this umbrella, from Christian practice to actual magic.

In thinking about reading as spirituality one cannot ignore the very deep roots that this organization has to Protestant practice and the ways this practice has historically been articulated in American civic life, particularly for women. It is important to remember that Protestantism spanned religious and secular worlds, meaning that it provided models for the organization of civic groups as well as for the church itself. The examples above demonstrate that the ties between the reading councils and their Protestant roots are still viable and that council members draw heavily upon their experiences and socialization as members of Protestant organizations to compose the practice of the reading councils and their ideas of reading. This is particularly so in relationship to the discourse of the spirituality of reading.

Chapter 9

Living Reading: Conclusions

Living reading means a way of thinking and acting through membership in a reading council, a world that names reading as its center. The activities of this world generate multiple meanings of reading, meanings which are related in complex ways to members' identities and work as educators. It is through these activities that members create the shared interpretive framework, which is the foundation for living reading.

Living reading, as the expression of the practices of the reading councils, is a dynamic, but ultimately conservative, concept. The preferred genres or forms of practice, although mutable, have been remarkably enduring. As a historical look demonstrates, many of the purposes and forms of council practice are borrowed from Protestant women's civic groups with roots over two hundred years old. These practices include, among other things, the form of business meetings, the emphasis on officers and minutes, and the linking of Protestant religious outlooks with educational concerns.

Although the ways that council members live reading are essentially conservative, new trends and ideas do find ways to enter council life. But they must be assimilated to the core of extant practices. The Howard presentation is a case in point. Howard borrowed many ideas from the emerging whole language movement but presented them not as part of a holistic outlook on language but as discrete technical elements—a moveable feast of ideas—that could be mixed and matched. Howard's approach to reading, as a set of technical elements or strategies, has its roots in the scientific reading movement. Ironically, she embeds this scientific or technological outlook toward reading in a revival format, drawn from the organization's Protestant roots. Howard's presentation is an excellent example of the kinds of layering and mixing that occur through the assimilation process. Indeed, this particular mixture of hybrid belief systems forms the distinctive style of the councils' outlook on reading.

Although council practice shifts and changes on the surface, there is a steady, continuous core of belief. First, and most important to members, is their shared passion for the teaching of reading and their belief in the importance that reading plays in today's world. Second is the role councils play in acknowledging, validating, and elevating the importance of teachers' work in teachers' own eyes and in the eyes of the community. And, third is the role that councils play as a spiritual outlet for teachers, providing them with opportunities for individual spiritual fulfillment and renewal and participation in the creation and nurturance of communities of colleagues. Each one of these three roles is closely intertwined. To believe that reading is all important is foundational to believing reading that teachers make critical contributions to society. Acknowledging and validating teachers' work provides teachers with fulfillment and renewal. Council participation, a shared communal activity, makes these experiences possible. Living reading incorporates aspects of belief, manner, and ideology as linked and reinforced through council practice, that is, the performance of these meanings.

In this study, I have paid special attention to two means by which these goals are achieved: (1) the genre of the expert presentation and (2) the discourse of the spirituality of reading. The expert presentation is the standard vessel into which the majority of council professional development opportunities are poured. The shape is so familiar to members that it could almost be said to be invisible to them, and yet it is a powerful force on the content of professional development and its possibilities. This genre absorbs many other forms and through it flow the words, symbols, and concerns of other communities of practice, other communities that serve as resources to the reading councils for content and form. An example of this process can be found in the notion of the discourse of the spirituality of reading.

Through the incorporation of discourses of spirituality with notions of reading, reading becomes a spiritual practice. To practice reading as spirituality, council members draw upon spiritual symbols, rituals, and knowledge present in our larger society, weaving these resources into statements that express their ideas about reading. This cobbling together of the spiritual with concerns about reading creates a new discourse, the discourse of the spirituality of reading, one that is ostensibly about reading but clearly speaks to many other issues, particularly teachers' roles and possibilities in schools and communities. The discourse of the spirituality of reading is not unique to the reading councils, but the strength of its meaning to council members and the ways in which they employ this discourse distinguish the councils from other national groups concerned with literacy issues.

The Reflexive Nature of Council Relationships

The councils, as communities of practice, are not isolated entities. They exist in overlapping relationship with numerous other communities of practice. Relationships among communities of practice are highly reflexive, which is to say that values and beliefs are constantly seeping back and forth across organizational and institutional lines and divisions. Two communities of practice, schools and publishers, exist in such close relationship to the councils that the connection can only be labeled symbiotic.

Councils and Schools

The purpose of councils' is directly related to that of schools' existence: the teaching of reading. Councils promote the work of teachers, and teachers are employed by schools. Council schedules coordinate with school schedules, and council events are planned to appeal to the needs of these school employees. Councils rely upon schools for a variety of supports, from meeting space and refreshments to xeroxing and mailing assistance. The language, symbols, and expectations of schools are deeply embedded in council life.

Those are the direct and easily perceived links between the two groups, but there are also subtle reflexive links that exist between councils and schools. These links throw light on some of the more complex issues of teachers' roles in education and, in particular, the gendered structuring of their position in schools. Examples of the more subtle reflexive links between schools and councils demonstrate how living reading is an aspect of living schooling. A good example of this is the way that council activities resemble what in schools are seen as enrichment activities.

School reading enrichment activities take several forms. They can be classroom based, including experiential activities and activities that allow children to pursue interests for pleasure. In highly structured classrooms even self-selection of reading books can be considered "enrichment." School enrichment activities may be organized school wide, such as field days, performances, carnivals, book fairs, etc. They may include the outside world, the "real" community penetrating the walls of daily school routine. This could mean community members reading to children in classrooms, authors and illustrators who speak to the group, and field trips to special sites or exhibits. What distinguishes enrichment from the core curriculum is that enrichment activities are seen as "add-ons." There is always the sense that if they were taken away, school, and the most important business of school, the transmission of the core curriculum, would continue.

Council activities mimic school enrichment activities to a high degree in both the form of the activities and the significance attributed to them. Presentations by outside experts and authors, carnivals of reading, and community service projects, such as are commonly found in council practice, are parallel to the sort of things seen in school as enrichment or additive activities. If we take this comparison one step further, then one could also say that council activities do not focus on the essentials. They circle, but do not touch, the core of what it is that schools and teachers are, or should be, about. This means that council work and the discourse of reading as foundational always exist in inherent contradiction to each other. On one side is the rhetoric about the absolute foundational nature of reading and the importance of the work of reading teachers, and on the other side is the nonessential nature of council members and/or elementary teachers'/women's efforts at autonomous, self-determining professional development.

Another example of the reflexive relationship between reading councils and schools (or the way that living reading is also a way of living schooling) is found in the way that the formal agenda of the reading councils parallels the official agenda of schools, while the operational agenda of the councils resists those very formal structures. In simplistic terms, schools' formal agenda emphasizes the informational, procedural, structural, and practical and de-emphasizes the expressive, aesthetic, spiritual, or interpretive. This is very similar to councils' formal agenda. Reading councils have charters, use parliamentary procedure, possess a hierarchical structure of officers—and all of this is virtually the same across the country. Their stated purposes focus on the informational (disseminating information about the importance of reading and research-based techniques for teaching) and the promotional (making everyone understand the importance of reading and helping the world come to enjoy reading). Council leadership, like school leadership, places great emphasis on problem solving, practicality, efficiency, and task orientation.

Yet this formal agenda differs significantly from the councils' actual operational agenda. After a hard day of work, few council members give up their evenings, leaving the dishes in the sink and the kids with their husbands, purely to hear what research says about reading. They are attracted by some other very important reasons as well. They want to be acknowledged, they want to be inspired, they want to be given hope that their work is contributing to a larger, significant, and meaningful goal. They want to be uplifted, to laugh, and to relax with others who really understand their world. They want to reexperience the "why" of why they went into teaching. The operational agenda of the councils then is to fulfill teachers' needs for spiritual self-fulfillment, expression, and communal identification. Reading then becomes an excuse or a vehicle for enlightenment or spiritual release. Not surprisingly, the most sought after speakers on the reading council circuit are those whose talks resemble a Christian revival.

Councils and Publishers

Schools form the primary institutional relationship with the councils, but publishers occupy a position nearly as important. Like the school-council relationship, the publisher-council relationship is also highly reflexive, but in very different ways.

The foremost way that publishers and councils are linked is that publishers want access to reading teachers as consumers and reading councils want financial and other material support for their activities. The promotion of publishing and related business enterprises is pervasive throughout the reading councils, from the local to the international level.

One of the most striking differences between the school-council relationship and the publisher-council relationship is that schools regard teachers as employees and publishers regard them as customers. As entrepreneurs addressing customers, publishers must understand the needs and desires of teachers in order to design their products, shape their publicity, and sell their products. Like ethnographers, publishers seek to understand the indigenous terms, concepts, and desires of this particular culture and to incorporate this understanding into their promotions.

For these reasons, publishers are quick to reflect what they think teachers want to hear. For instance, although textbook publishers were in the forefront of promoting the scientific reading approach objectified by the reading textbook, as whole language came to the fore and challenged this approach, publishers were quick to shift their tone. They began to use terms associated with the whole language movement in new versions of teacher manuals, added portfolio assessments to textbook packages, and incorporated "authentic literature" in their latest editions.

Publishers also build promotions based on their own notions of what teachers are and what they desire, notions reflective of society's assumptions about teachers. One of these assumptions is that teachers' and children's cultures are closely related and that both are embedded in the culture of schools. At the reading council conferences, many of the displays draw heavily upon popular images of the culture of childhood and the culture of schooling. Decorations may include gigantic stuffed teddy bears or school symbols such as red apples, yellow school buses, or little red schoolhouses. Publishing personnel may roam the floor in the costumes of storybook characters, handing out flyers to browsers.

Not only are participating teachers visually treated to childhood culture, but they are literally treated like children. Salespeople, serving like carnival barkers, urge them to participate in contests or have their picture taken with actors portraying storybook or media characters. Council members may scurry around from booth to booth getting salespeople to sign their chit so that they can prove they went to all the product areas in order to win a colorful tote bag.

The discourse of the spirituality of reading threads through publishers' promotions in many ways. It is present in the exuberant displays of materials that create the image of reading as a romantic, distanced world far away from the realities of public school. It is present in the messages about reading that can be found in promotional materials and blazoned on T-shirts, tote bags, and banners that publishers produce.

Council life is sandwiched between these dual spheres of activity—schools and publishing. The mission and purpose of the councils is an outgrowth and response to teachers' lives in schools. The councils are a place to acknowledge, praise, and expand members' contributions as reading professionals to schools. Ironically, councils are also places to resist the restrictions of schools and the boundaries they place on members' professional and spiritual potential. The concept of living reading, with its incorporation of spirituality with notions of reading, is both compliant and resistant to schools' agenda for teachers.

Publishers seek out councils in order to promote their products to members, and councils accept publishers' assistance as a means of supporting their activities. But the relationship is not that simple. Publishers are attentive to the ways that council members live reading, and they design promotions that play upon members' beliefs, desires, and goals, intertwining elements of the discourse of the spirituality of reading with the sale of their products. Publishers' sales pitches mix in other notions as well, injecting their beliefs about teachers, women, and children into the stew.

The discourse of the spirituality of reading is one of the ways that schools, councils, and publishers overlap, creating discursive links among these different spheres. Living reading requires that council members knit across these spheres, developing personal meaning from the integration of the various portrayals of reading that emerge at these different sites.

The Future of the Councils

In seeking to make my point that living reading is something very different from reading, that is, the act of deciphering text, some may conclude that I have come to the position that reading itself is unimportant. Nothing could be farther from the truth. I have worked with enough older beginning readers, both adolescents and adults, to understand what it means to be unable to read or to read with only halting fluency. If my own experience were not enough to convince me, there is increasing research evidence that, despite technological advances, reading is more, not less, important in today's world (Bruce 1998).

Given the increasing importance of reading, and the acknowledged flexibility of the structure of the reading councils, it is odd then to note that councils face serious challenges to their existence. At the time I completed this study, there had been an overall decline in membership, and leaders at all levels complained about their inability to attract younger, urban, and nonwhite members. There was concern that councils' traditional activities lacked appeal for potential new members. At all levels of the organization there had been increasing difficulty recruiting leadership.

Members speculated frequently on the reasons for these problems. They noted that teaching is an aging, shrinking profession and that districts provide more and more of their own staff development, meaning that districts are then less eager to have teachers take part in outside staff development. They were aware that school districts and universities were less supportive of faculty and administrator participation in council leadership roles than they once were. Council members complained that other issues have taken the place of reading in the public's imagination and in school politics. Now, instead of reading, districts are concerned with such issues as content standards and assessment, site-based management, and technology. Probably the most disconcerting issue for members is that they feel, as mentioned in the introduction, that no one can agree on what reading is. Competing paradigms vie for power in school districts and college reading departments and on national task forces.

Members feared that reading was declining as a driving force in education and as the identity of their professional organization, and they wondered what this would mean to their own sense of professional identification. Their fears about the status of reading were related to their sense that there had been a decline in respect for educational institutions and educators.

Implications of the Study

In thinking back over my experiences in the world of reading, I never cease to be amazed by the symbolic power of the notion of reading—the many meanings it has absorbed and the ways it has come to engage multiple communities. As a symbol, the notion of reading has shaped educational purpose and policy and the discussions surrounding these issues for most of the life of our nation. Taking reading as their central concern, the reading councils have, until recently, been situated at the symbolic core of educational life.

One of the primary purposes of the councils is the delivery of professional development to reading teachers, that is, the provision of information about research, strategies and approaches, materials, and policies that will support teachers to provide the best possible reading instruction. This study examines in detail the ways professional development opportunities are composed by council leadership, the traditional form these opportunities take, and the ways members experience professional development provided by the organization. Quite frankly, this close-up look at teacher-designed professional development contrasts sharply with many recent calls for professional development reform (Sparks and Hirsh 1997). It is one-shot, discontinuous, focused on product more than process, and allows little space for thoughtful reflection. It makes mincemeat of research findings, disparaging critical or rigorous examination of methods and findings.

What council practice does, as opposed to what it does not do, is provide a transnational forum for a vocational group, a deeply sought after and appreciated spiritual experience of vocation, and support for political action on the local level. These things are not inconsequential, but in the fuss and fury about meeting "prefab" educational reform designs their importance may go unrecognized.

As a professional organization, the reading councils, like other subject-area associations, are a forum for vocational identity. In David Hansen's eloquent discussion of teachers and vocation, *The Call to Teach*, he describes how "vocation emerges at the crossroads of public service and personal fulfillment" (Hansen 1995, 115). The call emerges and its response is shaped over time. Like an architect creating a home for a family, a teacher is constantly working in interaction with audience and materials to craft educational moments of integrity. Teaching requires great attention to the details of the task. The daily work is often accompanied by doubt and moral consternation, as teachers struggle to do right in conflicting, ambiguous, or even threatening situations. Teachers must daily take responsibility for the decisions they make in regard to children, colleagues, and community. They must accept the accountability that comes with working in the public sphere. When one has identified oneself as a teacher, one sees one's work as teaching, even when not directly engaged in the act of instruction. Members of the reading council often remark ruefully on this inability to stop teaching, even when they leave the classroom: Once a teacher, always a teacher.

The reading councils are a place where the vocation of teaching is recognized and celebrated. The councils link people who have accepted the call to teach, and in so doing they have defined reading as a key element of that commitment. Living reading, that is, participating in diverse council activities, is a means of acknowledging and renewing one's vocational commitment. It is also a place to recognize the difficulties of pursuing the vocation, the internal and external struggles teachers face in their work, and to gain support to soldier on.

One of the primary means by which council activities support and encourage teachers is through liminal or communal experiences, which are reflexive with their normal school lives. In expert presentations, and more comprehensive activities such as reading conferences, members enter liminal spaces in which normal expectations of time and space are disrupted. In these marginal zones, roles are reversed, taboo subjects enter the discussion, there is much playfulness and playing with boundaries. Powerful symbols, such as those combined in the discourse of the spirituality of reading, come into play. For teachers, who work in highly structured and often pressured settings, these moments of relaxation and renewal are extremely important. It is particularly meaningful for them that it takes place among a community of peers, people who face similar vocational issues.

In creating these liminal experiences, council members draw upon the dialogic and historical resources surrounding them. Just as the strength and endurance of the symbolic power of the notion of reading continues to surprise me, I also continue to be amazed by what I have learned through this study about the strength and endurance of Protestant forms of worship and civic involvement. Indeed, the importance of reading as a focus and symbol has much to do with the unique religious history of our country.

Criticisms of teachers, like criticisms of council practice, have focused on the lack of responsiveness to current reform goals. The councils are in many ways inherently conservative organizations, and yet in talking with members over the years I have found that, from their position as teachers, the reading councils are often the sole source of new ideas and support for the implementation of approaches deemed to be different and better educational practice. What this implies is that the average district may be far more impoverished, materially and intellectually, than we are ready to acknowledge and that the economic discrepancies among districts are a major factor impeding change.

Many of these districts operate on a shoestring budget. There is little extra funding for experimental purchases. Many council members must make individual requests of their school board for the small amount of funds necessary to attend the state conference. Thus, teachers lack professional development opportunities and so do their administrators. Lacking models and encouragement, local school cultures shy away from the kinds of intellectual engagement that current calls for reform envision.

Additionally, the majority of the council members with whom I became familiar work in communities that want their children to receive a recognizable and, thus, traditional schooling experience. Parents in these communities want their children to be happy with school and to do well, but they balk when school tasks begin to deviate far from what they experienced as schoolchildren. When this happens they worry that school may not be doing right by their child and that, lacking the basics, their child may not be able to perform well at the next levels. Few teachers can afford to risk their position through affronting local expectations, so they move carefully and incrementally to make changes they deem worthy.

Again and again I heard testimony from council members at all levels of the organization about the importance the council played in their teaching life, providing them with not only information about changing notions of reading instruction, but also praise for the fact that the councils simply existed and, by their existence, served to attest to the importance of these new ideas. Although members may feel isolated in their schools as they seek to make small changes in practice, at council meetings they feel the solidarity of the larger vocational group that is working toward the same end. This is not a small thing.

It is these teachers, the worker bees of our many school districts, who are in it for the long haul, upon whom the real weight of reform rests, and yet it is their voices, concerns, and experiences that often seem to be missing from so much of hoopla about educational reform.

But having made these statements in support of the councils, I cannot shirk from raising what were to me serious concerns. In particular, participating in council practice has led me to worry more about the role of women in education. In thinking about gender, I found that the councils are sites of complicity and resistance to gender restrictions. By celebrating the teaching of reading, councils celebrate elementary teachers, who are primarily female. They offer members chances for leadership, chances that are often lacking in schools. The friendship and solidarity that members gain through membership is highly feminine in nature: witness the reading sorority.

And yet, the hierarchy of council leadership often recreates the same gender hierarchy present in the schools. Women compose the bulk of council membership, but men are likely to move quickly and firmly into leadership positions. As in schools, women's reactions to the male preserve in the councils varies from awareness of gender manipulation and support of female friends to active support of male colleagues in defiance of female solidarity. Within the organization men tend not to be able to "see" the gender issue. Council activities themselves resemble many of the activities of traditional female civic organizations, as they also resemble the peripheral enrichment activities of school. I have to ask myself, What does it mean for women to center themselves ambivalently on the margins of power? How is this sense of ambivalence translated into school life and classroom practice?

In a related arena, participation in council practice raised concerns for me about the implications of the silences I encountered around issues of race, ethnicity, sexual orientation, and, indeed, any group or individual that could be classed as "other." It is true that on a formal level the organization has declined to support racist practices and on many organizational levels members work hard to promote a more diverse and multicultural curriculum in schools. At a deeper level, something like Chomsky's hidden grammar rules, there is a deep silence and discomfort with these issues. How, I thought, must the silence I feel be translated into classroom practice and discussions with students and parents, selections of materials, and the development of school policy in relationship to diversity? Knowing that the teachers within this organization represent the senior leadership of their schools, I wonder what it would take to make the acknowledgment and discussion of diversity a possibility in the schools in which they work.

Finally, as I think about the sources of thought that influence council members, I continue to be amazed by the power that publishers wield over council members' access to ideas about literacy and, as a consequence, the powerful ways that publishers shape educators' concerns about reading. In council life, publisher support makes possible many council activities, and publishers provide the majority of speakers whom council members hear at state and national meetings. Without this support, councils would not be able to provide the range of activities they offer, nor would the activities be at such reasonable cost.

In return for their largesse, however, publishers are allowed almost total access to council membership. Because of the reliance of the reading councils on publishers' financial support and good will, it may be difficult for members, particularly those in leadership positions, to question the ways that publishers may be shaping council agendas or the possible roles in curriculum development and professional leadership that publishers have usurped from educators.

Since the completion of this study the Internet has burst upon the educational scene. While many reading teachers were initially critical of computers in favor of old-fashioned books, the Internet has opened up vast new possibilities for literacy instruction and dissemination of curricular materials. Teachers and other nonprofit organizations can now be publishers in ways heretofore unimagined. Publishers are struggling to take advantage of the new media and stem the leaks in their own dykes.

Investigating Reading

Most studies about reading have been conducted in schools or in relationship to schools. By electing to study the reading councils, I chose a position that appeared to be at the margins of educational practice. In addition, by studying local practice as opposed to state or national practice, which by many people's standards would have had broader significance, I further distanced myself from expected norms for researchers. But to be at the margins and to be marginalized are two different concepts.

This study demonstrates that there is much potential for gaining valuable insights in educational studies if we seek out varied vantage points from which to consider educational concerns. For my purposes, voluntary professional organizations provided an exceptionally rich site for interpretation.

It is not only the variety of vantage points that are of importance here, but also the frameworks of interpretation that one applies. Different theoretical frameworks can lead to new and different questions. In trying to find an answer to "the paradox of reading" as it appeared to me, I had to temporarily abandon reading research and some of its traditional concerns. In so doing, I sought different theories and asked different questions.

Leaving Reading and the Reading Sorority

As is the nature of inquiry, through this study not only have I constructed "them," but, in the process, I have been constructing "myself." In trying to understand who "they" are as reading educators, I have come to better understand myself as a reading researcher (Rabinow 1977).

One of my favorite artifacts from this study is a photograph taken in our hotel room in Toronto during the 1994 IRA conference. We, the original reading sorority, are lined up in a row in the hotel's big double beds with just our heads poking over the covers. The picture is a little blurred so you can't see our grinning expressions clearly. This photograph expresses for me the delightful moments of lightness and the wonderful esprit de corps that women's worlds of friendship can bring.

At the same time that I have enjoyed the friendship and warmth of this world, however, I have retained my skepticism about various aspects of council practice: this tension remains. I did not come to this study as an evaluator or an investigative reporter. My task was to understand the ways that beliefs and ideas about literacy are formed and enacted through the practice of the reading councils. My investigations led me to examine what I have termed the paradox of reading and, subsequently, to my notion of living reading.

The notion of living reading and the theoretical discussions presented here represent my deep-seated concerns about the ways that we represent knowledge—bind it, package it, and distribute it. Through this work I hope I have made problematic some of the conventional ways we think about reading, at the same time suggesting directions for reconsidering those perspectives that may prove to be fruitful for future studies.

References

Adams, M. 1990. *Beginning to read: Thinking and learning about print* (Summary prepared by S. Stahl, J. Osborn, and F. Lehr). Champaign: University of Illinois, Center for the Study of Reading.

Anderson, R., E. Hieber, J. Scott, and I. Wilkinson. 1985. *Becoming a nation of readers: The report of the commission on reading.* Champaign: University of Illinois, Center for the Study of Reading.

Bakhtin, M. M. 1981. Discourse in the novel. In *The dialogic imagination,* ed. M. Holquist, 259–442. Austin: University of Texas Press.

———. 1984. Problems of Dostoevsky's poetics. Trans. C. Emerson. Minneapolis: University of Minneapolis Press.

———. 1986. The problem of speech genres. In *M.M. Bakhtin: Speech genres and other late essays,* ed. C. Emerson and M. Holquist, Trans. V. W. McGee, 60–102. Austin: University of Texas Press.

Bauman, B. and J. Sherzer, eds. 1991. *Explorations in the ethnography of speaking.* 2nd ed. Cambridge: Cambridge University Press.

Bergeron, B. 1990. What does the term whole language mean? Constructing a definition from the literature. *Journal of Reading Behavior* 22 (4): 301–329.

Bourdieu, P. 1977. *Outline of a theory of practice.* Trans. R. Nice, Cambridge: Cambridge University Press.

Bruce, B. 1998. Current issues and future directions. In *A handbook for literacy educators: Research on teaching the communicative and visual arts,* ed. J. Flood, S.B. Heath, and D. Lapp. Newark, DE: International Reading Association.

Buckingham, D., ed. 1993. *Reading audiences: Young people and the media*. Manchester, UK: Manchester University Press.

Chall, J. and J. Squire. 1991. The publishing industry and textbooks. In *Handbook of reading research, vol. 2*, ed. Barr, R., M. Kamil, P. Mosenthal, and P. Pearson, 120–146. White Plains, NY: Longman.

Connell, J. 1994. Reconstructing a pragmatic theory of knowledge: A transactional perspective. Ph.D. diss. University of Illinois, Champaign.

Daniels, A. 1988. *Invisible careers: Women civic leaders from the volunteer world*. Chicago: University of Chicago Press.

Darnell, R. 1991. Correlates of Cree narrative performance. In *Explorations in the ethnography of speaking*, 2nd ed., ed. B. Bauman and J. Sherzer, 315–336. Cambridge: Cambridge University Press.

Davidson, J. and D. Koppenhaver. 1993. *Adolescent literacy: What works and why*. 2nd ed. New York: Garland Press.

Dewey, J. 1934. *Art as experience*. New York: Perigee Books.

Edelsky, C. 1992. A talk with Carole Edelsky about politics and literacy. *Language Arts* 69 (9): 324–329.

Fairclough, N. 1992. *Discourse and social change*. Cambridge: Polity Press.

Foucault, M. 1972. *The Archaeology of knowledge and the discourse on language*. New York: Pantheon Books.

Gee, J. 1989. What is literacy? *Journal of Education* 171 (1): 18–25.

Goodman, K. 1992. Why whole language is today's agenda in education. *Language Arts* 69 (9): 354–363.

Graff, H. 1991. *The legacies of literacy*. Bloomington: Indiana University Press.

Grumet, M. 1988. *Bitter milk: Women and teaching*. Amherst: University of Massachusetts Press.

Hansen, D. 1995. *The call to teach*. New York: Teachers College Press.

Hansen, J. 1993. Discussion books for "Teachers as Readers" groups. *Reading Today* 10 (5): 35.

Hodge, R. and G. Kress. 1988. *Social semiotics*. Cambridge: Polity Press.

Illinois Reading Council. 1993a. *Illinois Reading Council conference program book*. Bloomington: Illinois Reading Council.

————. 1993b. *Membership statistics*. Bloomington: Illinois Reading Council.

————. 1994a. Budget report. Paper presented at the Illinois Reading Council Board meeting, Springfield, IL, April.

————. 1994b. *Bylaws of the Illinois Reading Council of the International Reading Association*. Bloomington: Illinois Reading Council.

————. 1994c. *Illinois Reading Council conference program book*. Bloomington: Illinois Reading Council.

International Reading Association. 1992. *IRA desktop reference, 1992–1993*. Newark, DE: International Reading Association.

Jerrolds, B. W. 1977. *Reading reflections: The history of the International Reading Association*. Newark, DE: International Reading Association.

Kaestle, C., H. Damon-Moore, L. Stedman, K. Tinsley, and W. Trollinger, Jr. 1991. *Literacy in the United States*. New Haven, CT: Yale University Press.

Kirsch, I., A. Jungeblut, L. Jenkins, and A. Kolstad. 1993. *Adult literacy in America*. Washington, DC: National Center for Education Statistics.

Knoblauch, C. and L. Brannon. 1993. *Critical teaching and the idea of literacy*. Portsmouth, NH: Heinemann.

Lankshear, C. and P.L. McLaren, eds. 1993. *Critical literacy: Politics, praxis, and the postmodern*. Albany: State University of New York Press.

Lave, J. and E. Wenger. 1991. *Situated learning: Legitimate peripheral participation*. Cambridge: Cambridge University Press.

Little, J. 1993. Teachers' professional development in a climate of educational reform. *Educational Evaluation and Policy Analysis* 15 (2): 129–151.

Long, E. 1993. Textual interpretation as collective action. In *The ethnography of reading*, ed. J. Boyarin. 180–211. Berkeley: University of California Press.

Luke, A. 1988. *Literacy, textbooks, and ideology: Postwar literacy instruction and the mythology of Dick and Jane*. Philadelphia: Falmer House.

Lutz, C. and J. Collins. 1993. *Reading national geographic*. Chicago: University of Chicago Press.

Martin, J. 1985. *Reclaiming a conversation: The ideal of the educated woman*. New Haven, CT: Yale University Press.

McLaren, P. (1986). *Schooling as a ritual performance: Towards a political economy of educational symbols and gestures*, 2nd ed. London: Routledge.

Moll, L., C. Amanti, D. Neff, and N. Gonzalez. 1992. Funds of knowledge for teaching: Using a qualitative approach to connect homes and classrooms. In *Theory Into Practice* 31 (2): 132–141.

Monaghan, E., and W. Saul. 1987. The reader, the scribe, the thinker: A critical look at the history of American reading and writing instruction. In *The formation of school subjects: The struggle for creating an American institution*, ed. T. Popkewitz, 85–122. New York: Falmer Press.

Myerhoff, B. 1978. *Number our days*. New York: Touchstone Books.

National Council of Teachers of English and the International Reading Association. 1996. *Standards for the English Language Arts*. Urbana, IL: National Council of Teachers of English.

Ong, W. 1982. *Orality and literacy: The technologizing of the word*. New York: Methuen.

Phillips, S. 1991. Warm Spring "Indian Time": How the regulation of participation affects the progression of events. In *Explorations in the ethnography of speaking*, 2nd ed., eds. B. Bauman and J. Sherzer, 92–109. Cambridge: Cambridge University Press.

Popkewitz, T. 1987. The formation of school subjects and the political context of schooling. In *The formation of school subjects: The struggle for creating an American institution*, ed. T. Popkewitz, 1–24. New York: Falmer Press.

Powell, W., ed. 1987. *The nonprofit sector.* New Haven, CT: Yale University Press.

Prose, F. (1999). I know why the caged bird cannot read: How American high school students learn to loathe literature. *Harper's Magazine* 299 (1792): 76–84.

Rabinow, P. (1977). *Reflection on fieldwork in Morocco.* Berkeley: University of California Press.

Radway, J. (1984). *Reading the romance: Women, patriarchy, and popular fiction.* Chapel Hill: University of North Carolina Press.

Reading Today staff. 1993. Fox blasts basals. *Reading Today* 10 (6): 17.

Rosenblatt, L. M. 1976. *Literature as exploration,* 3rd ed. New York: Noble and Noble.

————. 1978. *The reader, the text, the poem: The transactional theory of the literary work.* Carbondale: Southern Illinois University Press.

Rothman, S. M. 1978. *Woman's proper place.* New York: Basic Books.

Rousseau, J. 1979. *Emile or On education.* Trans. A. Bloom. New York: Basic Books.

Ruth, L. 1991. Who decides? Policymakers in English language arts education. In *Handbook of research on teaching the English language arts,* eds. J. Flood, J. Jensen, D. Lapp, and J. Squire, 85–109. New York: Macmillan.

Sanjek, R. 1990. On ethnographic validity. In *Fieldnotes: The makings of anthropology,* ed. R. Sanjek, 385–418. Ithaca, NY: Cornell University Press.

Scott, A. 1984. *Making the invisible woman visible.* Urbana: University of Illinois Press.

————. 1992. *Natural allies.* Urbana: University of Illinois Press.

Shannon, P. 1989. *Broken promises: Reading instruction in twentieth-century America.* Granby, MA: Bergin & Garvey.

————. 1990. *The struggle to continue: Progressive reading instruction in the United States.* Portsmouth, NH: Heinemann.

————. 1994. The social life of basals. In *Basal readers: A second look,* ed. P. Shannon and K. Goodman, 201–216. Katonah, NY: Richard C. Owen Publishers, Inc.

Shannon, P., K. Goodman, P. Crawford, C. Edelsky, and C. Murphy. 1994. In Basal readers: A second look. Symposium conducted at the annual meeting of the International Reading Association, Toronto, May.

Sklar, K. K. 1973. *Catherine Beecher: A study in American domesticity*. New Haven, CT: Yale University Press.

Smith, F. 1978. *Reading without nonsense*. New York: Teacher's College Press.

Sparks, D. and S. Hirsh. 1997. *A new vision for staff development*. Alexandria, VA: Association for Curriculum and Development.

Squire, J. 1991. The history of the profession. In *Handbook of research on teaching the English language arts*, eds. J. Flood, J. Jensen, D. Lapp, and J. Squire, 3–17. New York: Macmillan.

Star, S., and J. Greisman. 1989. Institutional ecology, "translations," and boundary objects: Amateurs and professionals in Berkeley's Museum of Vertebrate Zoology, 1907–39. *Social Studies of Science*, 19, 387–420.

Street, B. ed. 1993. *Cross-cultural approaches to literacy*. Cambridge: Cambridge University Press.

Turner, V. 1969. *The ritual process; Structure and anti-structure*. London: Routledge & Kegan Paul.

———. 1985. *On the edge of the bush: Anthropology of experience*. Tucson: University of Arizona Press.

———. 1986. Dewey, Dilthey, and drama: An essay in the anthropology of experience. In *The anthropology of experience*, ed. V. Turner and E. Bruner, 33–44. Urbana: University of Illinois Press.

Tyack, D. 1974. *The one best system: A history of American urban education*. Cambridge: Harvard University Press.

van Dijk, T. 1993. *Elite discourse and racism*. Newbury Park, CA: Sage.

Venezky, R. 1986. Steps toward a modern history of American reading instruction. In *Review of research in education*, ed. E. Rothkopf, 129–167. Washington, DC: American Educational Research Association.

Walmsley, S., and E. Adams. 1993. Realities of "Whole Language." *Language Arts* 79 (4): 272–280.

Wasser, J. 1998. *Technology infusion: A systemic proposition. Learning from the Hanau Model Schools Partnership.* Hanau Model Schools Partnership Research Brief #3, April. Cambridge, MA: TERC.

Wasser, J. and E. McNamara. 1998. *Professional development and full-school technology integration: A description of the professional development model of the Hanau Model Schools Partnership.* Hanau Model Schools Partnership Research Brief #5, August. Cambridge, MA: TERC.

Wasser, J., E. McNamara, and C. Grant. 1998. *Electronic networks and systemic school reform: Understanding the diverse roles and functions of telecommunications in changing school environments.* Hanau Model Schools Partnership Research Brief #4, June. Cambridge, MA: TERC.

Weedon, C. 1987. *Feminist practice and poststructuralist theory.* Oxford: Basil Blackwell.

Westbury, I. 1990. Textbooks, textbook publishers, and the quality of schooling. In *Textbooks and schooling in the United States, Part I,* ed. E. Elliot and A.Woodward, 1–22. Chicago: University of Chicago Press.

Studies in the Postmodern Theory of Education

General Editors
Joe L. Kincheloe & Shirley R. Steinberg

Counterpoints publishes the most compelling and imaginative books being written in education today. Grounded on the theoretical advances in criticalism, feminism, and postmodernism in the last two decades of the twentieth century, Counterpoints engages the meaning of these innovations in various forms of educational expression. Committed to the proposition that theoretical literature should be accessible to a variety of audiences, the series insists that its authors avoid esoteric and jargonistic languages that transform educational scholarship into an elite discourse for the initiated. Scholarly work matters only to the degree it affects consciousness and practice at multiple sites. Counterpoints' editorial policy is based on these principles and the ability of scholars to break new ground, to open new conversations, to go where educators have never gone before.

For additional information about this series or for the submission of manuscripts, please contact:

Joe L. Kincheloe & Shirley R. Steinberg
c/o Peter Lang Publishing, Inc.
275 Seventh Avenue, 28th floor
New York, New York 10001

To order other books in this series, please contact our Customer Service Department:

(800) 770-LANG (within the U.S.)
(212) 647-7706 (outside the U.S.)
(212) 647-7707 FAX

Or browse online by series:
www.peterlang.com